In Praise of Love

A PLAY BY

TERENCE RATTIGAN

WITH A CURTAIN-RAISER

BEFORE DAWN

HAMISH HAMILTON
LONDON

First published in Great Britain 1973
by Hamish Hamilton Ltd
90 Great Russell Street London WC1

Copyright © 1973 by Terence Rattigan

SBN 241 02486 2

822
RAT

PRINTED IN GREAT BRITAIN BY
CLARKE, DOBLE & BRENDON LTD
PLYMOUTH

In Praise of Love

All the above except the last two are available
in the three-volume *Collected Plays of Terence Rattigan*

For BINKIE,
and JOHN

AUTHOR'S NOTE

The plays are published in the order in which they were written, and in the order in which I had intended them to be performed. I was then thinking of *The Browning Version* and *Harlequinade* (*Playbill*, 1948), in which the insubstantial play successfully followed the substantial and an audience, moved by the first, seemed to be reasonably diverted by the second. During previews of *In Praise of Love* (first intended as a collective title to parallel *Playbill* and *Separate Tables*) we experimented with the order of running, and it was proved to the entire satisfaction of the director, John Dexter, and myself that the insubstantial should, on this particular theatrical occasion, precede the substantial. We both of us liked to think that the impact of the substantial on the audience was even stronger than that of *The Browning Version*. It is certain that they seemed in no mood for any subsequent frivolity, as with *Playbill* they had.

As a result the plays are now being performed in the reverse order, with *Before Dawn* serving purely as a truncated curtain-raiser to the play that was always intended to be the main part of the evening's entertainment and which is now, to avoid confusing our audiences, being performed under the original collective title : *In Praise of Love.*

October 1973   T. R.

In Praise of Love was first produced at the Duchess Theatre, London, on September 27th, 1973, with the following cast:

LYDIA CRUTTWELL	Joan Greenwood
SEBASTIAN CRUTTWELL	Donald Sinden
MARK WALTERS	Don Fellows
JOEY CRUTTWELL	Richard Warwick

The cast for *Before Dawn* was:

THE BARON	Donald Sinden
THE LACKEY	Don Fellows
THE CAPTAIN	Richard Warwick
THE DIVA	Joan Greenwood

Directed by John Dexter

Designer : Desmond Healey

IN PRAISE OF LOVE

Characters

LYDIA CRUTTWELL
SEBASTIAN CRUTTWELL
MARK WALTERS
JOEY CRUTTWELL

Setting: North London
Time: The present

ACT I

SCENE : A single light illuminates the face of LYDIA CRUTTWELL. *She is sitting, motionless, staring unseeingly into space. She remains so for some length of time.*
Then the lights come on and we are in the Cruttwells' flat in Islington, where LYDIA *is now found sitting motionless on a settee in the living-room.*
We see a small hall, large living-room, and part of a kitchen when the sliding doors are opened. A staircase—probably put in during conversion—runs from the living-room: first, up a few steps, to the kitchen (where the Cruttwells also eat), then turns sharply to lead to the room above. No window is needed, nor fireplace. The predominant feature of the room is books, for some of which there is no space but the floor, the book-cases having been stretched to their limit. There is a book-case even in the diminutive hall, and on top of that, looking incongruous, a man's white hat-box which once plainly contained a top hat, and may still. Other prominent objects are a small table on which some ordinary black and white chessmen are set out, plainly for use and not for decoration, a table bearing a tray of drinks, a sofa and various armchairs. The front door and hall are at the back and a door (R) leads to SEBASTIAN'S *work-room. From this is coming the sound of a typewriter being very intermittently used, with long pauses between short bouts, usually followed by unmistakable sound of angry erasure. It is about six o'clock of a spring evening. The time is the present.*
SEBASTIAN *comes out from his work-room, a cigarette between his lips, an empty glass in his hand, and spectacles over his nose.*

SEBASTIAN. Oh good, darling, you're back. The heating has gone wrong.
LYDIA. Has it? It seems all right in here.

3

She gets briskly to her feet and feels an ancient radiator.
Yes, it's on.
SEBASTIAN. (*At the book-case.*) It's icy in my room.
LYDIA *goes through the open door of the work-room.* SEBASTIAN, *left alone, pulls down a book and begins to search for some reference. Vainly. He puts that one on a pile near him and picks another. Same process.* LYDIA *comes out and quietly takes his glass from his hand.*
Oh thank you so much, darling—
She fills up his glass, a procedure she can carry out in her sleep.
LYDIA. You hadn't turned it on.
SEBASTIAN. What on?
LYDIA. The heat.
SEBASTIAN. (*Deep in a book.*) Really?
He says it as if it were a matter of the most breathless interest, a sure sign with him that he hasn't heard a word.
LYDIA *comes back with his glass.*
Oh thank you, darling. What kept you out so long? Oh, of course, old Doctor Ziegfeld. What did he say?
LYDIA. Ziegmann. He's very pleased indeed.
SEBASTIAN. What did I tell you? And you got held up by the bus-strike?
LYDIA. Not really. I found a new way on the Tube.
SEBASTIAN. (*Worried.*) Should you have?
LYDIA. Oh, it was quite easy—
SEBASTIAN. I meant isn't it a bit like strike-breaking?
LYDIA. Your social conscience would have preferred I walked?
SEBASTIAN. It's not all that far, is it?
LYDIA. About as far as Fleet Street—to which I notice you've had a hire-car the last three days.
SEBASTIAN. A hire-car is different.
LYDIA. Why?
SEBASTIAN. I charge it to the paper, so it's on their conscience not mine. Good. I've got what I'm looking for—which is a wonder. Darling, our books have got in the most terrible mess again.
He pulls a book out.
Norman Mailer in the poetry section. Why?
He throws it on to a chair.
And—I can't believe it—Sapper?

4

He pulls that one out violently and throws it on the ground.
That's for burning. Darling, couldn't Mrs. MacKintyre?
LYDIA. Mrs. Higgins. It hasn't been Mrs. MacKintyre for three months.
SEBASTIAN. I call her Mrs. MacKintyre.
LYDIA. She's noticed that.
SEBASTIAN *pulls out another book, clicking his teeth.* LYDIA *takes it.*
SEBASTIAN. Well couldn't *she*—?
LYDIA. No. She isn't, oddly enough, a trained librarian. She isn't a trained anything, come to that. She comes three times a week for two hours a day, never stops eating and costs a bomb.
SEBASTIAN. Is she worth having then?
LYDIA. Yes.
SEBASTIAN. I mean if she costs a bomb—
LYDIA. (*Loudly.*) She's worth having.
SEBASTIAN. A little tetchy this afternoon, are we?
He reaches up and grabs another book.
'Plain Talk About Sex'—next to Peter Pan.
LYDIA. (*Taking it.*) That's mine.
SEBASTIAN. For God's sake, why?
LYDIA. I bought it for a train, sometime.
SEBASTIAN. (*Taking off his spectacles.*) That doesn't answer my question. Darling, I mean, with your early life—
LYDIA. Perhaps it needed a bit of brushing up.
Pause.
SEBASTIAN. (*Blowing on his glasses, carefully.*) A criticism?
LYDIA. No. A comment. Where shall I put these books?
SEBASTIAN. In their proper sections. Where I suggest you might have put the others. You might go through them when you have a little time.
LYDIA. When I have a little time, it will be high on my list.
SEBASTIAN. You're in a stinking mood this evening, aren't you?
LYDIA. Am I?
SEBASTIAN. Was it what I said about your early misadventures?
LYDIA. (*Smiling.*) No, stupid. You of all people have the right to talk about that. I think it was what you said about 'criticism'. As if I would—
SEBASTIAN. But *you* said 'comment'.
LYDIA. There can be good comment as well as bad, can't there?
SEBASTIAN. In theory, yes. In fact, no. Remember, darling, that

5

you're speaking to a critic. You meant something a bit harsh by 'comment'. Oh yes. I know. Now, darling, you must realise—

LYDIA. You can't be expected to bash an old skeleton. I know.

SEBASTIAN. Darling, really! That wasn't very—tasteful, was it?

LYDIA. It was your taste. You said it.

SEBASTIAN. Then you shouldn't have remembered it. Not the actual *words*.

Looking at her.

Did I say skeleton?

LYDIA. Yes, I know. I've put on four pounds in the last four weeks. That's not an invitation—just a fact.

SEBASTIAN. (*In 'breathless interest' again.*) Have you? Have you really? Put on four pounds? Well, that's splendid—absolutely splendid. I mean it's marvellous news, isn't it. Marvellous.

He is looking at his book.

LYDIA. You hadn't actually noticed?

SEBASTIAN. (*Looking up from his book.*) Of course I'd noticed. I mean these last six months I've been watching you like a hawk.

Returning to his book.

I'm not so ignorant as not to know that putting on weight is the best sign of all. The conclusive sign you could call it.

LYDIA. Well, here's something even more conclusive. I was told by Uncle Constantin to show you this.

She takes a paper from her bag.

SEBASTIAN. Uncle—?

LYDIA. (*Giving him the paper.*) Doctor Ziegmann, I've told you a hundred times he was an old family friend from Tallinn—

SEBASTIAN. (*Holding the paper without looking at it.*) But not an uncle—

LYDIA. No. I just *call* him that. He's no connection. Just a fellow Estonian.

SEBASTIAN. Yes. He sounds it. I've never heard a thicker accent on the telephone. How long has he been over here?

LYDIA. As long as me. Twenty-eight years.

SEBASTIAN. As long as I, darling.

Looking at paper.

Of course *your* English is fantastically good, but you had a start on him, I suppose. I don't understand this at all. What is it?

LYDIA. It's a blood-test—my last one.

6

SEBASTIAN. (*Reading.*) Normal, normal, near-normal, normal, normal. Sounds like a very dull party—

LYDIA. (*Turning the page over.*) And there—under General Remarks.

SEBASTIAN. Dramatic progress fully maintained. Further weekly blood counts may be discontinued. Oh darling, isn't that marvellous!

He kisses the top of her head.

Isn't old Ziegfeld pleased?

LYDIA. I've told you—delighted. From now on I can lead an ordinary normal life. No dieting, no waggon, late nights—anything I like. Wants me to have a holiday, though.

SEBASTIAN. Oh yes, of course. Where are we now?—April. Well in three months time I'll take you somewhere we've never been before. Greece, if the Colonels have gone—

Back to his book.

I've lost my place now. Here it is. All right, darling. I'll be about half an hour—

He turns to his door.

LYDIA. You won't.

SEBASTIAN. Won't what?

LYDIA. Be about half an hour. Mark's due here five minutes ago.

SEBASTIAN. Mark? Mark Walters?

LYDIA *nods.*

He's in Hong-Kong . . . No, that's right. He's back. I spoke to him yesterday—

LYDIA. And asked him to dinner.

SEBASTIAN. On a *Thursday?* My copy day. I couldn't have—

LYDIA. You did. What's more you asked him to be sure and come an hour early.

SEBASTIAN. (*Explosively.*) Damn and blast! Why didn't you stop me? I remember now. I remember perfectly. You just sat there, with your vapid smile on, and did nothing—*nothing*—there's loyalty—

LYDIA. I thought you must have an easy one this week.

SEBASTIAN. Easy? *Easy?* Two sodding Professors on Shakespeare's imagery taking opposing points of view. Where *is* Mark?

He goes to the telephone.

In that hideous palace of his in Eaton Square—?

LYDIA. No. The workmen are there, adding something. He's at the Savoy.

7

Taking the receiver from him.
It's far too late, darling. With the bus-strike and the traffic he must have started an hour ago.
SEBASTIAN. Oh bugger!
LYDIA. (*Soothingly.*) Leave it to me. When he arrives I'll tell him you've got to meet a deadline. He's a writer too.
SEBASTIAN. *Too?* A writer is merely a euphemism, but 'too' is an insult.
LYDIA. Why? I wouldn't mind your selling a million copies before your publication date, and the film rights for half a million, sight unseen—
SEBASTIAN. I see. I see. So that's going to be thrown in my face. My novels sell five thousand and make me about seven hundred pounds in all—
LYDIA. Oh shut up! You don't write novels. I wish you did, but you don't—
SEBASTIAN *opens his mouth to speak.*
Twenty-five years ago you wrote a masterpiece, and followed it up four years later with another—
SEBASTIAN. No. The second was a mess—
LYDIA. It was as good as the first.
SEBASTIAN. It was a mess.
LYDIA. It was only that they all turned on you for not writing *Out of the Night* all over again. And so you gave up and joined the enemy. If you can't beat them, join them, I know, but you did give up a bit soon.
SEBASTIAN. Thank you very much.
LYDIA. My God, if Mark Walters took *his* notices as seriously as you did—
SEBASTIAN. His research staff and his stenographers and the man who writes the descriptive passages between bashes would all be out of a job. And Mark would still be a multi-millionaire. Oh God, the injustice of it all!
He holds out his glass for her to refill. She takes it.
Just take some power-mad tycoon with a permanent hard-on—
LYDIA. They're not all tycoons. His last one was about a Presidential candidate—
SEBASTIAN. With a permanent hard-on?
LYDIA. Semi-permanent. His son has the permanent one—he whams it up everything in sight.
SEBASTIAN. A wham a chapter as usual?

8

LYDIA. Sometimes more, but it averages out. Now the son meets a lion-tamer—

SEBASTIAN. Don't go on. Being fairly familiar with the author's 'oeuvre' I can catch the drift.

He looks towards his work-room.

I'll have to work late, that's all—and you know what that does to my bladder.

LYDIA. You finish now. Mark won't mind. I can delay dinner—

SEBASTIAN *nods gloomily and goes towards his door.*

Oh—talking of novels—

SEBASTIAN. We weren't.

LYDIA. I mean *your* novels. Darling are those notes for a new novel I came on in there the other day?

Pause.

SEBASTIAN. 'Came on' is good. 'Came on' is very good. I noticed that they'd been disturbed.

Roaring.

Is there *nothing* I can keep concealed in this house?

LYDIA. Oh—so you *concealed* them, did you? Why?

SEBASTIAN. Because I knew that once you got your X-ray eyes on them you'd be bouncing up and down, clapping your little hands and shouting: 'Oh goody, goody, he's writing a novel!'

LYDIA. Well goody-goody he is.

SEBASTIAN. No. Not necessarily at all. He may well decide to give it up, because it stinks, or decided that he hasn't got time for it anyway.

LYDIA. Oh, time isn't important. You can make that—

SEBASTIAN. What utter balls you do talk sometimes—

There is a ring at the front door.

Oh God!

LYDIA. You go in. I'll explain.

SEBASTIAN. No. I'd better say hullo.

LYDIA *opens the front door to* MARK. *He is in the early forties, and physically the exact opposite one would imagine, of any of his power-mad, randy heroes. He has a pleasantly mild expression and a weedy physique. He pants at the mildest physical exertion and is panting now. He carries two parcels under his arm.*

LYDIA. Mark, darling—this is wonderful—

She throws her arms round his neck.

MARK. Wonderful for me too. Let me get my breath back. Don't they have elevators in Islington?

SEBASTIAN. No.

MARK. Hell, lifts. As a resident I should remember. Hullo, Sebastian.

They embrace briefly.

Still murdering literary reputations?

SEBASTIAN. Yours is safe.

MARK. These days no one gives me notices. Even my friends on the *Cleveland Plain Dealer* who used to find me 'compulsive' now just says 'another Walters!'

SEBASTIAN. (*Snatching a parcel.*) Are these presents?

MARK. You've got Lydia's. This is yours.

LYDIA. Oh Mark, you shouldn't.

SEBASTIAN. Of course he should. It's his duty to redistribute his wealth. Mine rattles.

MARK. (*Snatching it from him.*) Then don't rattle it.

SEBASTIAN. As good as that, eh? I'll open it later, do you mind? I've got a little work to finish off. Lydia forgot it was my copy day—

LYDIA. *He* forgot.

MARK. Look if I'm a nuisance here why don't I take Lydia out for dinner and leave you to work—?

SEBASTIAN. And how do I get dinner?

MARK. Couldn't you scramble yourself some eggs?

SEBASTIAN. Are you mad?

MARK. Yes, I'm mad. For a moment I was thinking you were a normal husband.

SEBASTIAN. You look terrible.

MARK. I know. I always do.

SEBASTIAN. Why don't you look like your heroes?

MARK. If I did I'd write about heroes who looked like me, and I wouldn't sell.

SEBASTIAN. (*Having laughed.*) I often think if you'd had any education you might actually write.

MARK. If I'd had any education I'd know I couldn't.

SEBASTIAN. (*Kissing his cheek.*) I love you a little, do you know that?

To LYDIA.

Darling, fill this up, would you, and then get Mark a drink.

LYDIA *takes his glass again.*

10

MARK. How's Joey?

LYDIA. (*Eagerly.*) Oh he's doing wonderfully well, Mark.

SEBASTIAN. Wonderfully well? He has an unpaid job at the head-quarters of a crypto-fascist political organisation called the Liberal Party.

LYDIA. He's only unpaid now. After the bye-election they're going to pay him.

SEBASTIAN. Thirty pieces of silver, I should think.

To MARK, *tragically.*

Helping to split the left and let the Tories in. My own son, Mark. My own son!

LYDIA. (*Paying no attention.*) He's earned three hundred pounds, Mark, for a television play he's written. Isn't that marvellous? That's more than his father earned at twenty.

She gives SEBASTIAN *his drink.*

SEBASTIAN. The B.B.C. 2 series for which this piece of pseudo-Kafka crap was written, Mark, happens to be limited to plays by authors under twenty-one—

LYDIA. It's still an achievement—and you ought to be proud.

SEBASTIAN. Oh I am, very.

He sips his drink.

A touch too much water, darling.

LYDIA *angrily snatches the drink back.*

MARK. When's this play being done?

LYDIA. Tomorrow at 10.30.

SEBASTIAN. Prime viewing time.

MARK. I'll try and get to watch.

SEBASTIAN. (*In a murmur.*) Don't.

LYDIA. You wouldn't come and watch it here with us, would you? *She brings the drink back to* SEBASTIAN *having added whisky.*

SEBASTIAN. Darling, what a thing to ask the poor man!

LYDIA. It's only he could see Joey too. He's coming up from his bye-election especially to watch it with us. Don't you think that's rather sweet of him, when he could have seen it with his friends?

SEBASTIAN. I think it's wise. He knows we've got to like it.

LYDIA. Damn you, damn you!

She begins to switch lights on.

SEBASTIAN. Forgive her, Mark. She's been a bit hysterical lately.

LYDIA. Go and work.

SEBASTIAN. (*Soothingly.*) Yes, darling, I'm just going.
SEBASTIAN *goes to his door.*
LYDIA. Would you, Mark? I know it's an awful thing to ask but Joey would be thrilled out of his mind.
SEBASTIAN. Out of his what?
MARK. I'd love to.
SEBASTIAN. Good God.
He goes out.
MARK *faces* LYDIA. *There is a pause.*
MARK. Tell me please that I've come for no reason.
LYDIA. You've come, Mark, and I'm very grateful.
She kisses him fondly.
What do you want to drink?
MARK. (*Impatiently.*) Anything.
LYDIA. I went out and bought a bottle of Bourbon—
MARK. All right Bourbon. I want to see your latest blood-count—stop press.
LYDIA. (*Taking it out of her bag.*) But do you know anything about blood counts?
MARK. Since I got your first letter I had one of my research team—
LYDIA. (*Fondly.*) Darling Marcus Waldt. Darling, darling Mark Walters.
MARK. Hell, I'm not intelligent enough to research for myself.
He fumbles in his pocket and pulls out a notebook.
I told this guy it was for a character in a book. I got figures here—
LYDIA. For what?
MARK. (*Reading.*) Acute Lymphocytosis.
LYDIA. (*Handing him his drink.*) Say leukemia. It's a prettier word.
MARK. (*Harshly.*) I'm not taking self-pity from you yet.
LYDIA. Unkind, but justified. I drag you half-way across the world because I'm sorry for myself, and have to talk to someone. That's self-pity all right. I hope you had other reasons for coming?
MARK. (*Absorbed in his comparison of figures.*) What? Yes—plenty of reasons. These figures don't fit.
LYDIA. No.
MARK. They don't fit with—O.K.—leukemia.

12

LYDIA. No. Nor do they fit with the word 'normal' which dear Uncle Constantin has so sweetly typed in.

MARK. (*Studying another leaf.*) No. They're all above normal—

LYDIA. Quite a bit above?

MARK. Well—yes, I guess—a bit—

LYDIA. Then why did Uncle Constantin make them normal?

MARK. He wants to reassure you.

LYDIA. 'We are coming along most finely, my dear, improvink every day.' Uncle Constantin doesn't know I can see the tears behind those pebble glasses, and anyway they might be tears of joy, because we Estonians are an emotional people. I'm getting myself a drink.

MARK. Allowed it?

LYDIA. Encouraged, Marcus, encouraged.

She goes to the drink tray.

Vodka. American, but still vodka.

Impatiently.

Oh Marcus! Why am I being encouraged to drink, and lead a normal life, why am I being told I need no more blood tests, why am I being conned into thinking that I've had a dramatic recovery, when that test is worse than last week's, and considerably worse than the week's before?

MARK. How did you get to see your tests?

LYDIA. I told you—I pinch them.

MARK. How?

LYDIA. Each week I have to spend a penny for a specimen. I tell him I can't do it with someone in the room, even behind a screen.

After a sip.

Oh God. It doesn't even *taste* like vodka. Still, press on. Anyway the old boy discreetly disappears and I rifle his desk. I've a good head for figures. Nowadays I don't even need to write them down.

MARK. (*Indicating the paper and his notepaper.*) Why are these figures lower than mine?

LYDIA. Cortisone. Lashings of cortisone. What Uncle Constantin has told me are my little tonic pills.

She opens her bag and takes out a bottle, shaking two into her hand.

Which reminds me.

She takes them, swallowing them with vodka.

13

Two six times a day now. It was two four times a day until last week.

MARK *snatches the bottle from her hand.*

MARK. Where does it say they're cortisone?

LYDIA. Nowhere.

MARK. How do you know then?

LYDIA. Analysis at an ordinary chemist. 'Oh Miss—could you help me. I've found these in an old bottle and I'm not too sure what they are . . . Oh how kind . . . Cortisone? Fancy. That's a powerful drug isn't it? I'll throw them away—'

A sudden slight access of tears. She embraces him.

Oh Marcus, I'm so happy to see you. I'm such a stranger in this land. Even after twenty-eight years I haven't anyone—anyone whom I could call a friend.

MARK. That's hard to imagine.

LYDIA. Well I could have had lovers—but after—after what Sebastian's just called my early misadventures—aren't English euphemisms wonderful? I didn't want them. But a real friend, no. Among the other refugees I suppose I could have made some, but that would have meant swapping concentration camp stories, probably in front of Sebastian, who dreads them. But so do all the English. Do the Americans?

MARK. Some, I'd say—the ones who ape the English. Easterners. But, hell, you *are* speaking to Marcus Waldt, Lydia. Grandfather Lithuanian Jewish. Most of us Americans *are* refugees. Not necessarily from concentration camps—but from something like them. Not as bad—but still bad. No, mainly we sympathise.

LYDIA. In this country I learnt my lesson early. At first, when I had an even stronger accent than now, people would politely ask me where I was from, and I'd say Estonia. Then I could see them thinking : 'Now where the hell is that? Oh yes. Baltic States. Germans *and* Russians. Jesus, we'd better not ask her *her* experiences.' But some did, and I'd be silly enough to tell them.' and I'd see the glassy stare of utter boredom in their eyes. And something worse—I was guilty of bad form—especially if, as I sometimes did, I cried a bit when telling. Oh damn the English ! Sometimes I think that their bad form doesn't just lie in revealing their emotions, it's in having any emotions at all. Do you like the English?

MARK. I don't quite dig them. But I like their country. So I live in it rather than mine.

14

LYDIA. Yes I like their country too, and sometimes say so—and that's bad form too. No, Mark, in England I'm very alone. Of course I have Joey—but even he gets embarrassed if I even hint at what I feel for him. As for—

She jerks her thumb despairingly at SEBASTIAN's *room.*

No. I think I should have gone away with you when I had the chance.

MARK. I think you should too. Among other things, it would have saved me two sets of alimonies.

LYDIA. And *you* I could have told I was dying of leukemia.

MARK. No, Lydia. If that was true, mind you—*I* would have told you. At the proper time. Not till necessary. Not till you had to know. But the doctor and I would have been in league from the start.

LYDIA. Yes. Well, perhaps there are some English husbands who'd have behaved the same way. It's difficult for me to say. I've only really known one. I'm getting another drink. What about you?

MARK. (*Shaking his head.*) Sebastian might have behaved the same way, if you'd given him the chance.

LYDIA. (*Laughing.*) He'd have tried to, poor lamb. For a week or two he'd have remembered his upbringing at Winchester and Balliol. Manners Makyth Man. And for a week or two he'd have been quite solicitous—'Do lie down, old girl. Mustn't tire yourself, you know. I'll get you your tea—"

She laughs.

Just to hear that I sometimes almost wish I *had* told him. But after a time, can you imagine the boredom he'd have gone through? Don't fool ourselves, Mark, a long, slow terminal illness is the worst visitation we can inflict on anyone, let alone our nearest and dearest. And Sebastian isn't the best person in the world at being bored. The glassy stare, very soon, and then going on for months and months. Then, when I came to die I wouldn't have enjoyed looking up into Sebastian's face—and seeing relief. This is morbid. Let's talk of something else. Hong-Kong—

MARK. Not yet. There's still leukemia. There's no certain proof until—

LYDIA. (*Interrupting.*) I've had the lumbar puncture.

MARK. (*Looking at his notebook.*) Now would that be the sternum test?

15

LYDIA. Yes. I had it yesterday. It was positive.

MARK. The result wouldn't be through.

LYDIA. No, it isn't, officially. But Uncle Constantin's nurse is Scandinavian. Accent very like mine. I called the hospital, got the specialist's secretary, said Doctor Ziegmann needed a verbal report and couldn't speak himself as the patient was in his consulting-room at that moment. She swallowed it. Said she'd look it up—

MARK. Where were you?

LYDIA. In a call-box, scared to death it would sound off before she found the report. It didn't. 'Mrs. Lydia Cruttwell—Positive.' Very brisk voice. No, 'I'm sorry.' Just 'positive'. Now you'll have another drink?

MARK. Yes.

LYDIA *takes his glass.* MARK *jumps up.*

No, you sit down. I'll—

LYDIA *laughs.*

LYDIA. Don't be silly. Cortisone makes me feel eighteen again. It's a wonderful drug. They dope racehorses with it. Honestly, I've never felt better.

MARK. There's a man in Denver Colorado who guarantees a seventy per cent cure.

LYDIA. (*Laughing.*) Denver, Colorado!

MARK. There's no money problem.

LYDIA. I know. There's no Marcus problem. There's just a Sebastian problem. And that, darling Marcus, is insoluble.

MARK. He's got to be told sometime.

LYDIA. When the ambulance comes. Perhaps not even then. Certainly not before.

MARK. If this test really *is* positive, your doctor will tell him.

LYDIA. Oh no, he won't. Uncle Constantin promised me most sacredly—a long time ago.

MARK. I could tell him.

Pause.

LYDIA. (*Quietly.*) And guarantee my never speaking to you again —ever, in this life.

MARK. Christ, Lydia—he's your husband.

LYDIA. No. Oh yes, I have my marriage lines written in Russian with a British Occupation Authority stamp on it, but Sebastian didn't take me for better, for worse, in sickness and in health, to love and to cherish. He took me to give me a passport—

16

MARK. For other reasons than that, for Christ sake.

LYDIA. Two, if you like. I made him enjoy going to bed with me, because I'd learnt how. And sometimes, in those early days, my funny English made him laugh. And a third. I fell in love with him at once, and never really fell out—not even now. So he felt under an obligation. Still when we got to England we were supposed to divorce. But gradually I made myself too useful to him to be got rid of. Deliberately, Mark. Deliberately. Then we had ourselves a son—

She stops suddenly and bites her lip.

Oh God—Joey—

MARK *is beside her, holding her tight.*

MARK. Lydia, darling, you must let me help you. You mustn't give up—you mustn't—please—

SEBASTIAN *puts his head round the door.*

SEBASTIAN. Darling, my special reading light doesn't go on.

Neither MARK *nor* LYDIA *show any embarrassment at their intimate attitude.*

Darling, I said my special reading light—

LYDIA. I heard you. What's the matter with it?

SEBASTIAN. (*Simply and reasonably.*) It doesn't go on.

LYDIA. Probably the bulb.

She goes past him into the room.

SEBASTIAN. Do forgive me, Mark. Just two more sentences. You haven't been too bored, I hope.

MARK. Not at all. What are you writing on this week?

SEBASTIAN. That complacent old burgher of Stratford-on-Avon. God, he's so maddening. With his worship of the Establishment he makes nonsense of everything we write, don't you think?

MARK. *We?*

SEBASTIAN. (*Appalled.*) Are you a *Republican*?

MARK. (*Hastily.*) Gee no. I'm a radical—

SEBASTIAN. Well Shakespeare *must* infuriate people like us who passionately believe that no man can write well whose heart isn't in the right place.

MARK. Meaning the left place?

SEBASTIAN. (*Feeling his heart.*) Which is where the heart is. Thank you, Mark. I might use that as my pay-off.

LYDIA *appears.*

Well?

LYDIA. It wasn't plugged in.

SEBASTIAN. Who unplugged it. Mrs. MacKintyre?

LYDIA. (*Gravely.*) Probably Mrs. MacKintyre.

SEBASTIAN. You must speak to her, darling. Set up the chessmen, Mark.

He goes into his room.

There is a pause.

MARK. Now who on earth is going to look after that, if—

LYDIA. Say 'when', Mark. Get used to it, please.

MARK. (*Stubbornly.*) I'm not saying 'when', Lydia. I'm sorry. Someone's got to keep a little hope going around here. You seemed to have resigned yourself to black despair—

LYDIA. Black despair? Me! Marcus, have you forgotten, who you're talking to? Black despair! Me. Between the ages of sixteen and twenty-two I had to face, every day and every night, the almost certain prospect of death in a hundred really horrible ways. Thirty years later I face a very gentle kind of death—

She knocks on wood.

well, let's hope. But my books aren't frightening about it at all, and they give me about eighteen months. Eighteen months? That's a long time. And then—'To cease upon the midnight with no pain'? God, how many millions of us over there during those six years longed for just that—and didn't get it. Black despair! Me! Marcus, really!

MARK. I'm sorry. Only I'd sooner not talk about it too much, if you don't mind.

He pulls one of his parcels out and begins to open it.

LYDIA. Well, we've got to talk about it a little or you're not going to be much of a help, are you?

MARK. O.K., but not now. Do you mind?

LYDIA. Just one thing more. You asked a question and I've got to answer it.

MARK *is taking out a set of very beautiful, carved, Chinese chessmen, in red and white, and is methodically replacing the black and white pieces with them on the table in the corner.*
LYDIA, *obsessed with her problem, has not yet noticed what he is unobtrusively doing.*

Who's going to look after *that*,

She thumbs at SEBASTIAN'S *door.*

when *I* can't any more. Well I've an idea—

MARK. I suppose he couldn't just look after himself?

LYDIA. Are you mad?

MARK. Hasn't he ever *had* to? Surely in the war—

LYDIA. Commission in Army Intelligence at once, and a batman. Knowing him, probably two. What are you doing over there?

MARK. Don't look yet. How does he reconcile all that with his Marxism?

LYDIA. Surprisingly easily. No, I've got an idea. There's a girl called Prunella Larkin—a journalist, who's mad about him, and I gather rather his form too, mentally *and* physically. Anyway he's been seeing an awful lot of her recently. In fact I think for the last three months they've been having a thing—

MARK. So? He doesn't seem to have things much—

LYDIA. Unlike you sex-maniac.

MARK. Don't confuse *me* with my heroes.

LYDIA. You do all right.

MARK. What makes you think it's a thing?

LYDIA. Well he's not a master of subterfuge. He takes this Larkin out to dinner—a little business chat, you know, darling—and later gets caught in the rain when there isn't any, and stays the night with his Editor who sends him a postcard the next day from Tangier. You know the form.

MARK. Who better? Only mine don't go to that much trouble. They just sleep out and when I ask where, it's mental cruelty.

LYDIA. Now the doctor says I must have a holiday. Will you take me away for ten days?

MARK. Sure. Where?

LYDIA. Ilfracombe's nice—

MARK. So's Monte Carlo. What's this to do with Miss Larkin?

LYDIA. Mrs. Larkin, divorced. Well he'll say 'who's going to look after me?' And I'll say 'what about that nice girl Prunella'—and he'll jump at it. Then if the ten days are a success—well, later on, I can make plans accordingly.

MARK *is silent.*

Don't you think it's a clever idea?

MARK. I can only repeat what Sebastian so often says to you : you are an extraordinary woman. All right. Now you can look.

He carries the completed table over to the centre of the room.

LYDIA *looks in wonder.*

LYDIA. (*Picking up a piece.*) Oh but these are exquisite.

MARK. Chinese. Nothing very grand. Modern.

19

LYDIA. But they're beautiful. He'll adore them. My God, if his is as good as that, I'm going to open mine.

She snatches up the remaining parcel and begins furiously to unwrap it.

MARK. Listen—if that doesn't suit—

LYDIA has managed to open the parcel which is a box and peers inside, past tissue paper. Then she closes the box.

LYDIA. No. Take it back.

MARK. Lydia.

LYDIA. Take it back this instant.

But she holds on to it firmly. There is a pause. Then gathering strength, she whisks out a silver mink wrap. She gazes at it lovingly.

I said—take it back.

MARK. I heard you.

He takes the wrap from her and holds it out for her to slip into. She does so.

LYDIA. I didn't mean a word of what I said just now. I think you're an absolute horror.

MARK. Yes.

LYDIA. Flaunting your wealth, showing girls what they've missed by not divorcing their husbands and marrying you.

She looks at herself from every angle in the mirror. Then she gives him a passionate embrace. Finally she takes his empty glass.

MARK. Well, maybe I sensed this was special.

LYDIA. Special it was. Thank you, dear Marcus.

She embraces him again. SEBASTIAN comes in.

SEBASTIAN. Have you two nothing better to do? You're not even giving the poor man a chance to smoke.

LYDIA. I haven't seen him for six months.

SEBASTIAN. Nor have I. Nor has anyone. Darling, that lovely patent folding table of yours doesn't fold—

LYDIA. (*Looking in the room.*) Well, of course, it doesn't if you leave the typewriter on it.

She flaunts her wrap in front of his eyes, to no effect whatever. Crossly she goes into the work-room.

SEBASTIAN. (*Very half-heartedly after her.*) Oh darling—do let me—

He takes half a step to the work-room, and three or four full and determined steps over to the drink tray.

20

MARK. Finished?

SEBASTIAN. More or less. I've fixed both the Professors, and the Swan is sunk in his own Avon without a trace.

MARK. Never to rise again?

SEBASTIAN. Ay. There's the rub. One has to admit that the bloody old honours-hunting bourgeois could write. William Shakespeare, Gent. Hard to forgive him for that. It should have stamped him a forgettable nonentity for the rest of creation. Instead of which—

MARK. Didn't you get something?

SEBASTIAN. An C.B.E.

With rage.

Lydia forced me into that. She staged a sit-down strike.

MARK. Isn't an C.B.E. what's called an honour?

SEBASTIAN. I would rather not speak of it, if you please.

He slips into the chair opposite MARK, *facing him across the chessmen. He picks up a white pawn in one hand, and a red one in the other.*

Now, are you prepared for your usual thrashing?

MARK *taps his left hand.* SEBASTIAN *opens it, revealing a red pawn.*

Good. There is no question at all that I am better playing red than—Red?

He picks up his pawn again, feels it lovingly and then stares at the whole board. Then without a word he gets up, crosses to MARK *and gives him a full, fervent kiss on the mouth.*

I passionately adore you, and am prepared to live with you for the rest of my life.

He picks up more pieces to feel them.

What is more I take everything back that I've ever written about your novels.

MARK. You've never written anything about my novels.

SEBASTIAN. Your next one will get my whole three columns—

MARK. I think I'd rather have a kiss.

SEBASTIAN *has sat down again.* MARK *has moved a piece.*

Pawn to Queen four? Ah. You've been reading your Fischer-Spassky—

MARK. You know something, I'd give a million bucks to write one novel a tenth as good as your *Out of the Night.*

SEBASTIAN. So would I. Only I haven't a million bucks.

Picking up his King and Queen to fondle them.

21

These are marvellous. Of course you can't tell the King from the Queen, but when can you these days?

MARK. Are you never going to try another novel?

SEBASTIAN. That'd be telling.

MARK. Good. That means yes.

SEBASTIAN. No. You said 'try'. I've got to be *moved*, Mark. The war did move me and that novel was good. It wasn't Tolstoy like some idiots said, but it was good. Then the Peace didn't move me, and that novel was bad.

MARK. No.

SEBASTIAN. (*Belligerently.*) Listen, who's the critic here?

MARK. Sorry.

SEBASTIAN. But I'm not beyond hope about the next—if I do it. Ah.

Referring to the game.

The Queen's gambit. I thought you'd grown out of that—

MARK. I've got a new variation—

SEBASTIAN. You'll need it. My reply to the Queen's gambit makes strong men quake—

LYDIA *comes in and moves ostentatiously about in front of* SEBASTIAN—*showing off her wrap.*

Darling, can you leave the ashtrays till later? It's a bit distracting, all that moving about.

LYDIA *stands still, with a sigh.*

Oh by the way—do you see what Mark's given me?

LYDIA. I'm trying to show you what Mark's given me.

SEBASTIAN. (*Looking up at her.*) Oh, what?

After a pause.

Oh that.

Another pause. To MARK.

What fur exactly is that?

LYDIA. (*Explosively.*) Don't tell him!

Savagely.

Dyed rabbit.

SEBASTIAN. Mink? I see.

Pause.

Very nice.

Pause.

Isn't that light shade just a bit—forgive me, darling—on the young side—?

Before he has finished LYDIA *has slipped the wrap off and has*

22

swung it at his head, disturbing several chess pieces. Out-raged.

Darling, really. These are valuable—

He and MARK *pick up the pieces.* LYDIA *goes to sit down in a sulk, hand on fist, staring at her husband with hatred.*

I'd just moved pawn to King 3.

Holding a pawn.

Superb workmanship.

He allows MARK *to re-arrange the board.*

Where did you get them?

MARK. Hong-Kong.

SEBASTIAN. Of course.

A horrifying thought strikes him.

Oh Mark, I may have to give them back. All that sweated labour—

MARK. Imported from Pekin.

SEBASTIAN. (*With a deep sigh of relief.*) Ah. Good.

MARK. It's all right if they sweat in Pekin?

SEBASTIAN. They don't sweat in Pekin.

MARK. Or they'd be arrested.

SEBASTIAN. Please don't make cheap jokes like that, do you mind? Now. Your move.

They have re-arranged the board. LYDIA, *after a questioning glance at* MARK, *fills up her own glass.*

LYDIA. Sebastian, Mark wants to take me down to Monte Carlo for ten days or so—

SEBASTIAN. What for?

LYDIA. A holiday. A rest—like the doctor said—

SEBASTIAN. Well, can't you have a rest here?

LYDIA. Since you ask—no. Unless you go to Monte Carlo instead.

SEBASTIAN. Well that might be an idea. I doubt if my Editor would scream with joy though, seeing he's away too.

LYDIA. In Tangier.

SEBASTIAN. Yes. How did you know? Well, can you get Mrs. MacHiggins to come in every day?

LYDIA. Not a chance.

SEBASTIAN. Just as well. It'd be very expensive.

LYDIA. But I've got a better idea. I haven't asked her, but I think I might just get Prunella to look after you.

SEBASTIAN. Prunella? Prunella Larkin?

LYDIA. Yes. Just for that little time.

23

Pause.
SEBASTIAN. Are you round the bend?
Letting himself go.
There is no such thing as a little time with Prunella Larkin.
An hour is an eternity. Ten days—ten *consecutive* days with her
and I'd be a gibbering lunatic.
LYDIA. (*Not displeased.*) Oh. It's just that you did seem to have
been seeing quite a lot of her recently—
Pause.
SEBASTIAN. (*Carefully.*) Mrs. Larkin and I do, I grant, have
certain interests in common, but they are interests that can
usually be shared in well under thirty minutes. If after those
brief encounters I should choose not to plod back to Islington
but to sleep in my editor's flat, to which I have a key, that is
a matter for my conscience but not for your prurient suspicions.
If you insist on skipping off on this extravagant jaunt, I shall
go to the Savoy and send the bill in to Mark. If he doesn't pay
I shall sell these chessmen. Now, does that settle the
matter?
LYDIA. (*A shade breathlessly.*) Yes. Oh yes. Oh yes, it does.
SEBASTIAN. Good.
Gravely.
Your move, Mark.
LYDIA *suddenly bursts into a peal of slightly drunken laughter
and kisses his head.*
Darling, please. This game needs concentration. Bobby Fischer
won't have a camera click ten yards away—much less a hyena
screeching tipsily in his ear.
LYDIA. Sorry. I was trying to kiss you.
SEBASTIAN. There is a time and a place.
LYDIA. Yes. I know both.
*Trying to be very silent, she puts down her glass, fumbles in her
bag and takes out two pills from the familiar bottle. In doing so
she knocks a glass over.*
SEBASTIAN. Darling, go and cook dinner.
LYDIA. Yes.
She swallows the pills with a sip of vodka.
MARK *sees her.*
MARK. (*Sharply.*) You've already had two of those—
LYDIA. Yes, but I missed two after lunch.
SEBASTIAN. What's she had two of?

24

LYDIA. My tonic pills.

SEBASTIAN. (*Deep in thought.*) Oh yes, those iron things. Very good for her, Mark. Put on eight pounds—

LYDIA. (*Shouting.*) Two!

MARK *castles.*

SEBASTIAN. The move of a coward.

After a pause.

How did we get to know each other, Mark? It was in California when I was lecturing at U.C.L.A., but I don't remember exactly how—was it chess?

MARK. No, it was Lydia.

SEBASTIAN. Oh yes, of course. You thought you were in love with her then, didn't you?

MARK. (*Looking at* LYDIA.) I think I still am.

SEBASTIAN. (*Deep in the game.*) Extraordinary.

LYDIA *picks up her wrap to have another go, but is warned by* MARK *with a gesture.* SEBASTIAN *looks up.*

Oh are you still there, darling? I thought you were getting dinner.

He makes his move.

LYDIA *determinedly finishes her vodka, pours another and carries it to the stairs with her, which she surmounts with caution.*

LYDIA. Something tells me your dinner tonight might taste a little peculu—peculiar.

MARK. (*Rising.*) Can I help?

SEBASTIAN. (*Roaring.*) Sit down, Mark. It's your move.

MARK *moves but keeps his hand on it.*

LYDIA *from the kitchen door gestures* MARK *to sit down.* SEBASTIAN *looks up at her as she opens the door, her back to him. She goes inside.* SEBASTIAN *looks down at the board again. There is a long pause.* SEBASTIAN *leans back abstractedly. Murmuring.*

Ay, but to die and go we know not where;
to lie in cold obstruction and to rot;

MARK *who has been about to make a move stops with his hand on the piece, staring at* SEBASTIAN.

This sensible warm motion to become
a kneaded clod; and the delighted spirit—

Are you making that move?

MARK. I don't know yet. Is that Shakespeare?

C   25

SEBASTIAN.
To be imprisoned in the viewless winds,
And blown with restless violence round about
The pendant world!
Can't keep your hand on it for ever, you know—as the Bishop
said to the actress—
MARK. O.K. That's my move.
SEBASTIAN. And a bloody silly one too, if I might say so.
He considers, and then continues softly.
The weariest and most loathed worldly life
That age, ache, penury and imprisonment
Can lay on nature, is a paradise
To what we fear of death.
Yes, Shakespeare. One is forced to admit that he could some-
times sort out the words. Pessimistic old sod!
MARK. I thought he was a complacent old bourgeois.
SEBASTIAN. He was both—that's the trouble.
He moves.
This move will lead to your ultimate annihilation.
MARK. The Cruttwell variation? It has interest, if only fleeting.
He considers the board.
What made you choose that particular quotation?
SEBASTIAN. Hm?—Oh, it's in my article. The same man that
wrote those lines also wrote :
We are such stuff as dreams are made on,
And our little life is rounded with a sleep.
The first one is Royal Court, but that one is pure Shaftesbury
Avenue. Cosy, commercial and comforting. Man wasn't con-
sistent, you see. . . . (*Muttering.*) Gent. . . .
MARK. (*Making a move.*) Check.
A key turns in the front door and JOEY *comes in. His hair is long,
but neat: his sweater and slacks are of sober hue. He looks what
he is, a Liberal. He carries an overnight bag.*
SEBASTIAN. (*Not seeing him.*) I think you have fallen right into my
trap.
JOEY. Hullo, Dad.
Pause. Neither smile.
SEBASTIAN. Are we expecting you?
JOEY. No.
With warmth.
Hullo, Mr. Walters.

26

MARK. (*Getting up and shaking hands.*) Hullo, Joey. You look ten years older than when I last saw you.

JOEY. I feel ten years older. You don't know what canvassing in a bye-election can do to one.

He puts down his bag.

SEBASTIAN *contents himself with an abstracted Pah!*

MARK. Congratulations on getting a play done on TV, Joey. That's great.

JOEY. I'm scared to death. Anyway, ten thirty. No one'll see it. No hope of you seeing it, is there?

MARK. Sure. I'm coming here tomorrow just for that.

JOEY. (*Awed.*) Specially to see my play?

MARK. Yep.

JOEY. Jesus—

MARK. I'm sure it'll be great—

SEBASTIAN. (*Loudly.*) Do you mind not yakkety-yakketing with my vote-splitting son? You are playing chess with me.

JOEY. Who's winning?

SEBASTIAN. I have him in a trap. It's only a question of how best to snap together it's steel jaws.

JOEY *examines the game.*

JOEY. Looks the other way round to me.

SEBASTIAN. (*Snarling.*) Do you mind?

JOEY. Sorry.

SEBASTIAN *puts his hand on a piece.* JOEY *hisses gently.* SEBASTIAN *withdraws it. Then he put his hand on another piece* JOEY *hisses again.*

SEBASTIAN. Will you kindly cease your imitation of a cobra on heat? Faulty though it may seem to budding Empire Loyalists, I prefer my game to *be* my own.

JOEY. I just didn't want to see you lose your Knight.

SEBASTIAN. (*Who plainly hasn't seen.*) My Knight?

JOEY. Two moves ahead—

SEBASTIAN. (*After a pause.*) Now a Knight sacrifice might well be my plan. How do you know it isn't, eh?

Nevertheless he withdraws his hand.

after a moment he makes another move without hesitation.

JOEY. That's torn it.

SEBASTIAN. (*Explosively.*) If you're so bloody good, why don't you ever play?

JOEY. I do.

27

SEBASTIAN. I meant with me.

Pause.

JOEY. Two reasons, I suppose. One, you don't ask me. Two, if I did win you'd call me a fascist pig.

SEBASTIAN. Meaning I'm a bad loser?

JOEY. Meaning that anyone who stamps on your ego is always a fascist pig.

SEBASTIAN. Go away, or I'll stamp on something more painful than your ego.

JOEY. I want to watch. You don't mind, do you Mr. Walters?

MARK. Not at all.

SEBASTIAN. (*Calling.*) Lydia! Lydia!

She comes out of the kitchen.

The brood is here. Remove it before I do it violence.

LYDIA. (*With a joyous cry.*) Joey!

She begins to run down the stairs. Thinks better of it and waits half-way down for him to bound up to her. There they have a warm embrace.

Joey! Oh, how marvellous!

She embraces him again.

SEBASTIAN. (*To* MARK.) Forgive her, Mark. She hasn't seen him for five days—

LYDIA. Why didn't you let us know? Have you eaten?

JOEY. Yes. I only knew myself at the lunch break. They don't need me until Election Day—

LYDIA. Thursday? And I've got you till then?

Joey nods. SEBASTIAN *looks up at them.*

SEBASTIAN. I've got him too.

JOEY. Don't bother, Dad. I won't be in *your* way.

SEBASTIAN. Not till Election Day? Ha! That must mean your man's given up.

JOEY. He's got it made, Dad. The latest poll gives him twelve per cent over all other candidates.

SEBASTIAN. I don't believe it.

Rising to get a drink.

The electorate, God knows, can be utterly idiotic, but it's not raving mad.

LYDIA. (*To* JOEY.) Could you get your mother a little sip of vodka, dear?

JOEY. I didn't know you drank vodka.

LYDIA. I've rather taken to it in the last hour.

28

She sits carefully on the steps.

JOEY *comes down into the room to get her her drink.*

SEBASTIAN. It doesn't make sense. It's all Bernard Levin's fault.
Centre Party! What in hell is a Centre Party?

JOEY. (*Gently, as to a child.*) A party that's in the centre : that's
to say, between the two extremes—of right.

He demonstrates
and left.

He demonstrates.

The two are now close at the drink cupboard.

SEBASTIAN. Don't talk to me as if I were a cretinous ape who
only involved himself in politics yesterday—

JOEY. No. It was quite a long time ago, wasn't it, Dad? When
Hitler was the devil, Stalin was in his heaven and all was right
with the world. Times have changed you know. You old-time
Marxists are out of touch.

He takes the vodka up the stairs to his mother.

She strokes his hair.

SEBASTIAN. Out of touch, are we?

LYDIA. (*To* JOEY.) Careful dear.

To SEBASTIAN.

Did you ever have hair as beautiful as this?

SEBASTIAN. Much more beautiful. But I was in an army, fighting
Fascism, and I was made to cut it short. That was for hygiene.
Lice.

JOEY. Did you get many lice as an Intelligence Officer in White-
hall?

*He has sat two steps down from his mother who seems bent on
stroking his hair and whom he is never averse from having do
so.*

SEBASTIAN. I was speaking figuratively.

JOEY. Figurative lice?

LYDIA. (*Hastily.*) Don't annoy him. You know what'll happen.

SEBASTIAN *to* MARK, *with sudden venom.*

Are you going to take all night?

MARK. (*Startled.*) Sorry.

He makes his move.

JOEY. You're out of touch, dad. It's all talk. You really don't want
action any more. We do, you see—

SEBASTIAN. Flashing mirrors in the eyes of South African
cricketers?

29

JOEY. We didn't do that. But we did get the tour stopped. And what did you do, Dad? Booked tickets for the Lord's Test.

SEBASTIAN. (*Roaring.*) Don't flout the issue! A Centre Party is nothing more nor less than gross collaboration with the enemy.

LYDIA. (*Happily sipping.*) Collaboration. That's very bad. We used to get shot for that—first by the Russians, then by the Germans, then by the Russians again. It was all very confusing.

JOEY. (*Patting her hand.*) Mum, that was a long time ago.

LYDIA. Yes, it was. It sometimes doesn't seem so.

JOEY. (*To* SEBASTIAN.) I suppose by 'the enemy' you mean the status quo.

SEBASTIAN. (*Looking at board.*) What?

To JOEY.

I mean the whole, rotten stinking mess that is Britain as it is today.

JOEY. What, mum?

LYDIA *is whispering in* JOEY's *ear.*

SEBASTIAN. What's she saying?

JOEY. She says 'Isn't it terrible, but she rather likes Britain as it is today.'

SEBASTIAN. She's pissed.

JOEY. (*Laughing.*) Are you, Mum?

LYDIA. Well, it's not a very nice way of—

Firmly.

Yes, I am.

JOEY. Good for you.

JOEY. (*Getting up from the steps.*) Dad, I'm not denying that all of us today, on both sides of the Atlantic, are living in a nightmare. But we want to *do* something—

LYDIA. (*To herself.*) Nightmare—

She titters, still happy.

SEBASTIAN. Darling, are you going to sit there just repeating everything we say?

LYDIA. (*Defiantly.*) Yes, if I want to.

SEBASTIAN. You don't think a touch of light cooking might be in order?

LYDIA. I like this discussion.

SEBASTIAN. Well you're not making a great contribution to it.

LYDIA. How can I make a contrib—join in your discussion? I don't belong to this country.

JOEY. Mum, you do.

30

LYDIA. No. I'm an Englishwoman—thanks only to the lucky accident of a British Intelligence Officer having a night-out in the Russian Zone of Berlin, and stopping off at Bentinck Strasse sixteen.

SEBASTIAN. For God's sake, Lydia, Joey mightn't know we met in a whore-house.

LYDIA. Well, he does now.

Daintily.

And anyway I've always called it a 'Maison de Rendezvous'.

JOEY. (*To* SEBASTIAN.) Don't worry, Dad, I knew where you met Mum.

SEBASTIAN. Good. But it's not a thing to go roaring from all the roof tops in Islington.

LYDIA. I was not roaring it from all the roof tops in Islington. I was simply trying to remind you—all you Anglo-Saxon gentlemen—that I was born and bred in a country called Estonia, which doesn't any longer exist. (*To* SEBASTIAN.) Now England still does—by some miracle—

SEBASTIAN. (*To Mark.*) Forgive the refugee bit. She doesn't do this often—

LYDIA. And England—taking it all in all—hasn't, over the last (*Trying to remember.*) twenty-eight years—that's right—twenty eight—been too bad a place for an Estonian to have lived in. I shall now go and cook.

SEBASTIAN. Yes, darling. Good idea. (*To* MARK) I don't know what's come over her, I'm so sorry, Mark.

JOEY. (*Smiling.*) To *have* lived in, Mum? Why? Are you planning to leave?

SEBASTIAN. (*To Mark.*) Do you really want me to take that pawn?

LYDIA *suddenly clutches* JOEY *in a fierce embrace. He is surprised.* LYDIA *recovers quickly.*

LYDIA. (*In a 'matter of fact' voice.*) I mean't up to now, Joey, of course. (*She turns, takes a step or two quite firmly away from him, then staggers and seems likely to fall. Surprisingly, it is* SEBASTIAN *and not* JOEY *who is by her side to prevent her falling.*) (*To* SEBASTIAN.) I'm pissed, aren't I?

SEBASTIAN. As a newt, I would say. (*To* MARK, *who is already by his side.*) Better take her up to bed . . . No, there's no need to carry her. I've tried it. She weighs a ton. (*To* LYDIA.) Just put one foot after the other, dear—That's right. It's called walking. Well done—clever girl. Joey, your mother has plainly passed

31

out for the night, and unless someone is prepared to do something about it, we will all be going without our dinner. . . .
JOEY *goes towards the kitchen.* MARK, *meanwhile, is helping* LYDIA *up the stairs.*

JOEY. I'll do what I can.

SEBASTIAN. That's a good boy. (*He reaches the table.*) (*Calling.*) What was your move, Mark?

MARK. (*By this time off.*) Pawn to King's Rook three—

SEBASTIAN. (*At the table.*) Yes . . . I thought it was (*He sits down.*) *The lights come down until only his face is visible. Then all the lights go out.*

ACT II

FIRST VOICE. (*Simultaneously.*) Well, I can only repeat what I've just said. . . .
We now can recognize the voice as the warm and friendly one of Vic Feather's.
it's the government's responsibility to govern. . . .
A light comes on to illumine JOEY'S *face as he kneels beside a TV.*
but a bad law is still a bad law, whatever governments' in power. . . .
JOEY *turns the control down to silent.*
JOEY. (*Calling.*) Mum!
LYDIA. (*From the kitchen.*) Yes, darling?
JOEY. What will they all be drinking?
LYDIA. (*From the kitchen.*) Leave that to me.
JOEY. O.K.
LYDIA *appears from the kitchen with a tray on which is a bottle of champagne and three glasses.*
LYDIA. This is what they'll be drinking.
JOEY. Oh Mum. That's making too much of it.
LYDIA. You can't make too much of it.
She has honoured the occasion with what is, perhaps her best cocktail dress.
JOEY *takes the tray from her.*
Nervous?
JOEY. Petrified. Why only three glasses?
LYDIA. Darling, if you forgive me, I think I'll stick to Vichy water.
She sits down, exhausted.
That ought to go in a bucket. There's one in the kitchen. Put quite a lot of ice in it. It's been in the fridge—but it'll look better.
JOEY. How are you feeling now?

33

LYDIA. American vodka is terrible stuff. Now if it had been Estonian vodka—

JOEY. You'd probably be dead, instead of just dying.

LYDIA *throws the quickest of glances at him, but is reassured by his grin.*

LYDIA. Very likely. Go and get that ice.

JOEY. And another glass—

LYDIA. All right. Just a sip, in your honour.

JOEY. (*Looking at his watch.*) You don't suppose Dad's forgotten, do you?

LYDIA. Of course not. He's been talking of nothing else all day. Go on.

JOEY. Where is he?

LYDIA. They wanted him at the office. An obituary or something. He'll be well on his way back by now.

JOEY. Did you call him?

LYDIA. Yes. He said he'd be back in plenty of time.

JOEY. Good.

He runs up the stairs.

LYDIA. And Joey—

She makes the correct sign.

Merde.

JOEY. (*Smiling.*) Thanks.

He goes into kitchen.

The second he has gone LYDIA *is on her feet, walking quickly and silently towards the telephone. She looks up a number in a private book, then dials with speed.*

LYDIA. (*Into receiver.*) Mrs. Larkin?—Lydia Cruttwell. I'm sorry to be embarrassing, but this is a crisis. Is Sebastian with you? — I see. When did he leave?—That's over an hour ago. Where was he going?—Please, Mrs. Larkin, this isn't a jealous wife. I'm not jealous—I'm pleased, really. But this is important, dreadfully important.—No clue at all? Did he happen to mention that his son had a television play on tonight?—Yes. B.B.C. 2, 10-30—Thank you—Yes. Only twenty—thank you. Yes, that's the crisis—Something worse? What *could* be worse? —Well, he sometimes goes to his Editor's flat after—talking with you. Did he say anything?—Meet some friends? Where? —Well, what's his favourite haunt up your way? After your flat, of course—

Her face grows despairing.

But I can't ring all those. Please try and help. I've got to find out where he—

She stops abruptly as JOEY *appears with the bucket and an extra glass. Laughing gaily.*

Oh, that's terribly sweet of you, darling—angelic of you to ask us, but I know Sebastian can't. He gets so tied up in the evenings—it's when he works you know—

She smiles happily at Joey.

I'll get him to call you. He's due in any second. Goodbye.

To JOEY.

What a bore that woman is!

JOEY. Who?

LYDIA. No one you know. An old woman called Lady Robinson.

Always trying to get us out for cocktails—

JOEY. I didn't hear the telephone ring—

LYDIA. That happens to me when *I'm* getting ice.

The doorbell rings. Distractedly.

That's Mark. Answer it darling.

JOEY *runs to the door.* MARK *is outside. He has graced the evening with a dinner jacket.*

MARK. (*Shaking hands.*) Well, Joey, here's wishing you everything.

JOEY. Gosh, Mr. Walters, you didn't change for me?

MARK. Of course. Always dress for a premiere. Here's a little sprig of heather for luck—

The sprig of heather is fairly easily recognisable as a small Cartier box. MARK *comes into the room and kisses* LYDIA.

Evening, Lydia.

LYDIA. (*Gratefully.*) Marcus.

They kiss. JOEY *meanwhile is opening his present. They are cufflinks.*

JOEY. Are these cuff-links?

LYDIA. (*Looking at them.*) No, they're ear-rings, and they're meant for me.

To MARK.

What are you trying to do, Mark? Keep the whole Cruttwell family?

MARK. Well, this is a very important occasion—the début of a brilliant young dramatist.

JOEY. Dramatist—gosh—you don't get called dramatist till you're dead.

35

LYDIA. He let 'brilliant' pass.

JOEY. No I didn't, Mum. I just closed my ears.

Engrossed in his cuff-links.

I don't think I've ever had a present like this.

Belatedly.

Of course Mum's given me some smashing things—

LYDIA. (*Arm around him.*) Smashing. Nickel cigarette lighters, plastic Indian beads. Joey's going to look after Sebastian while we're away—

MARK. That's great.

JOEY. If you don't mind putting it off until after next week-end. I'm going to stay with our candidate and his family for a victory celebration.

MARK. Hadn't you better knock on wood?

JOEY. No.

LYDIA. Isn't it sweet of him to volunteer to be my replacement?

JOEY. I didn't volunteer, Mum. You had your thumb-screws squeezed really tight.

LYDIA. Joey—that's a very naughty thing to suggest—

JOEY. Anyway we don't know what Dad's going to say.

LYDIA. (*Firmly.*) Yes, we do. He said this morning that he was very impressed with how you took over last night, when your mother got a little—er—over-excited. He said the way you coped in the kitchen was excellent.

JOEY. I know how to open a tin of sardines, and where the chocolate biscuits were kept—

LYDIA. (*Firmly.*) An excellent meal, he said.

MARK. And he washed up brilliantly. I would have helped but our game went on till two. That guy's like Churchill. He will never surrender.

JOEY. (*Laughing.*) He did last night, though. Gosh, did he roar!

MARK. And he blamed the new chessmen, of course. They confused him.

Pointing to the work-room.

Is he in there?

LYDIA. (*Calmly.*) No.

Looking at her watch.

He's due in any minute.

To JOEY.

36

Don't you think you should wear those cuff-links—for luck?

JOEY. I haven't got a shirt—I mean for links.

LYDIA. Borrow one of your father's.

JOEY. (*Slightly dismayed.*) Does that mean a tie?

LYDIA. Oh no. Don't betray your convictions.

JOEY *bounds up the stairs and off.* LYDIA *instantly becomes tense.*

Mark, Sebastian's lost. It's a hundred to one he's forgotten—

MARK. Oh God, no—

LYDIA. Go down to the porter. He lives at number 75, in the basement. He's got a telephone. Call this number—

She is hustling him towards the door.

I'll tell Joey you're reparking your car, or something—

MARK. What shall I say?

LYDIA. You don't need to say anything. I'll do the talking. Wait a moment.

She runs to the desk, takes out an envelope and scribbles on it. Then she gives it to him.

Is that clear. My hand is so shaking with rage—

MARK. (*Reading.*) 'Sebastian—If after 10.30 go away until well after eleven. And then, the first thing you say is "Congratulations, Joey". I'm covering for you.'

LYDIA. Not even *he* can fail to follow that, can he?

She opens the door, licks the flap of the envelope, and sticks it to the door.

MARK. He can do some funny things.

LYDIA. You see how I'm laughing in anticipation.

JOEY *comes running down the stairs, wearing a shirt much too large for him, outside his slacks. For* JOE's *sake.*

Tell the traffic warden you're a foreigner, Mark. That always works—wait—here's the latch-key—

She gives him a key and then closes the door quickly in his face. To JOEY.

Americans always park their cars in the middle of the street.

JOEY. He won't miss anything?

He looks at his watch. LYDIA *coming calmly towards him slaps his hand.*

LYDIA. Plenty of time, dear. Don't fuss. You want me to fix these for you?

JOEY. Yes, please. They're complicated.

LYDIA *attends to fixing the links.*

Your hands are shaking, too.

37

LYDIA. Well, of course, I'm nervous—
Pause.
JOEY. Are you sure Dad hasn't forgotten?
LYDIA. Positive.
JOEY. I hope he's not late. If you miss the beginning it's difficult
to follow.
LYDIA. His opinion means a lot to you doesn't it?
JOEY. Well—after all—one of the best critics in the world—Gosh!
They glitter. Look.
LYDIA. Yes. You have to flash them around a bit—preferably
under a light.
She shows him how with her bracelet.
I think the shirt in, don't you? Otherwise it looks a bit like a
night-dress.
JOEY. O.K. The one thing against going on living here, Mum is
—well—Dad.
LYDIA. You mean a lot to him, Joey.
JOEY *laughs, not unkindly.*
JOEY. Oh Mum. No one means a lot to him, and you know it.
Not even you.
LYDIA. Joey, that's a bad thing to say.
JOEY. Yes, it is, but it's the truth. And one has to tell the truth,
LYDIA. Has one?
JOEY. Honesty in this life is just about the only thing that matters.
LYDIA. Is it?
JOEY. (*Impatiently.*) We both know that the only person who
matters to Dad is Dad. Mum—you've admitted that to me
often enough—
LYDIA. As a joke, perhaps.
JOEY. No, as the truth. Don't be dishonest, Mum, please.
LYDIA. I'm sorry. It's only—well, I still think *you* mean some-
thing to him—something special—
JOEY. Mum, he can't wait for me to get out of this house. He's
said so often enough.
LYDIA. He doesn't always mean what he says—
JOEY. He means that. I agree he doesn't mean a lot of other things
he talks about—like politics. He only spouts Marxist Revolu-
tion as a kind of spell to prevent it happening—like some people
talk about death. You know the kind?
LYDIA. Yes. I sympathise a bit—
JOEY. (*In full spate.*) I think it's dishonest to spout a theory when

you personally would hate it coming true. Imagine Dad being ordered by his State-Controlled British Sunday paper to say that Evelyn Waugh was a bad writer? Or that Orwell was a lackey of the bourgeoisie? He'd be in a labour camp in a week.

LYDIA. (*Gently.*) I believe these days it's a mental home.

Pause.

JOEY. Of course, your father and brothers died in a labour camp, didn't they?

LYDIA. As far as we know.

JOEY. I'm sorry.

LYDIA. Don't be. It's all past. All you're saying, Joey, is that your father has the courage of his convictions—

JOEY. If they're about literature. About politics he just talks meaningless slogans. Sorry, Mum. Now I'm grown up I'm answering back, and he hates it. It won't work. I know it won't. Mum. I'm sorry. I can't stay on. It isn't possible. If it was just you—

He squeezes her hand.

But it isn't.

LYDIA. You don't think the ten days—?

JOEY. If we get through them without actual bloodshed it'll be a miracle—

The telephone rings. LYDIA *flies to answer it.*

LYDIA. (*At telephone.*) Hullo—oh hullo, darling. We were getting worried. Where are you?—You're going to watch it there—with the editor? You mean he's going to watch too?

JOEY. Gosh! Is it colour?

LYDIA. Is it colour, Joey wants to know?—Very latest, of course . . . I'll give them to him for you . . . Yes. See you afterwards.

She rings off.

He wishes you everything, Joey.

JOEY. The Editor!

He speaks as if God had announced he would be viewing.

It might get written about—

LYDIA. That must be Dad's hope, I suppose.

JOEY. Gosh! Jesus!

LYDIA. You see—he does think of you sometimes.

JOEY. Surprise, surprise!

Suspiciously.

I bet that was your doing.

LYDIA. (*Startled.*) What?

39

JOEY. I bet you made him get his Editor watching.
LYDIA. No, it was entirely his own idea.
JOEY. Ha, ha.
LYDIA. Are you saying I'm a liar?
JOEY. Well—I bet you used pressure.
LYDIA. Now, Joey, what pressure have I ever been able to bring on your father to do something he didn't want to do?
JOEY. There you are. You're admitting it.
LYDIA. What?
JOEY. That he's a selfish old brute, and impossible to live with.
LYDIA. (*Sharply.*) Joey, I won't have you talking about your father like that—do you understand!
JOEY. Yes, Mum.
LYDIA. Especially after this—very—generous thing he's doing for you tonight. Going all that way up to the city—
JOEY. (*Embracing her.*) Yes, I'm sorry. I'm sorry.
LYDIA. (*Still trying to be angry.*) And getting his Editor—
JOEY. Yes, I know, I know. I'm sorry.
Pause. LYDIA *looks down at his head, resisting the temptation to stroke it.*
LYDIA. (*Bravely.*) I know that during those ten days, you're going to find out a lot more about him—
JOEY (*His voice muffled on her shoulder.*) Oh God, I hope not.
LYDIA. (*Shaking him.*) Joey! I mean what he's really like.
JOEY. I know what he's really like.
LYDIA. Well—so do I, and I've lived with him happily for twenty-eight years—and will for the rest of my life.
JOEY. (*Releasing himself.*) Not necessarily. You never know. Someone else might come along—
LYDIA. No one else will come along.
JOEY. Well, anyway, it's different for you. You're married to him. I'm not.
LYDIA. No. You're just his son.
JOEY. Mum—that might have been some argument in Victorian times. It's not now.
LYDIA. No, it's not. Now we know it's healthy for sons to turn against their fathers, and we encourage it. But, Joey, we also know that sons have always turned against their fathers, all through history. Sebastian turned against his—
JOEY. The Bishop?
He laughs.

40

Yes. I feel sorry for the Bishop—
He bends down to put the television on.
Just warming it up. Oh God! Supposing there was a fuse—
LYDIA. I'd mend it. And the Bishop revolted against his father, who was a city swindler, of enormous charm I believe. Before that there was a drunken farmer, and what father he turned against I don't know.
JOEY. (*Still at the television.*) What does all this prove?
LYDIA. The enormous importance in life of pretending—
JOEY. (*Upright.*) Pretending to like someone one doesn't? I'm sorry but I can't do that.
LYDIA. Have you tried?
JOEY. No, because I think it's wrong.
LYDIA. Why wrong?
JOEY. It's dishonest.
LYDIA. Take Mark. When a writer of his standing gives up a whole evening to come out to Islington to see a half-hour's first play by a twenty-year old acquaintance, and puts on a black tie and says something pleasant about the début of a brilliant young dramatist—isn't there some pretence in that? Or is honesty so damn important for you that you'd rather he'd stayed home and done what he really wanted to do tonight?
Pause.
JOEY. (*Unhappily.*) What's that?
LYDIA. I don't know. But a pleasure-loving multi-millionaire mightn't be lost for something other than driving through a traffic jam out to Islington for a sandwich and a half-hour's telly.
Pause. She has shaken JOEY.
JOEY. He's older. I can't do things like that. Besides Dad, of all people, would laugh in my face.
LYDIA. I don't think so.
JOEY. My God, I've tried—well—politeness you'd call it—
LYDIA. No, I'd call it manners. It's an old-fashioned word and I'm sorry. But there isn't a better one.
JOEY. (*Scornfully.*) Manners makyth Man?
LYDIA. Yes. And it makyth other men feel better—as it's made you tonight.
JOEY. Well, I've tried it. With Dad sometimes. When he's written a good article, for instance. And what do I get always? A kick in the teeth—

D   41

LYDIA. Manners—real manners—means slipping your teeth into your pocket and pretending you're not hurt. It also means trying to feel some understanding for the man who kicked you.

JOEY. Sounds like a gooey sort of ultra-Christianity.

LYDIA. There isn't any sort of *ultra*-Christianity. There's just Christianity. And if it's gooey—well, it's gooey.

JOEY. I didn't know you were religious.

LYDIA. It's wonderful how that word today is made to sound like some curious perversion—permissible, of course, like all things, but rather unmentionable. Yes. I was brought up a Catholic—

JOEY. You don't go to *church*?

LYDIA. Oh no. What *would* the neighbours say? I haven't been to Mass since before the war. Neither the Russians nor the Germans were exactly Jesus freaks—and—well—one gets out of things. But somehow I still—oh no arguments, Joey—least of all on theology. Not now. Not at this moment—

Looking at the set.

Isn't that a bit green?

JOEY. No. The faces are right.

Violently.

Mum—if he'd only once lose an argument, say he was wrong, say he was sorry—

LYDIA. Yes, yes. I know.

MARK *comes in, panting.*

MARK. I know my next present to you, Lydia. Only it won't be a present to you, it'll be to me. A simple hoist is all that's needed—labelled for Mark Walters only. I'm on time anyway, aren't I?

JOEY. Yes. Two minutes.

MARK. Good. I wouldn't have missed a word.

JOEY *is looking at him, puzzled, appreciative and rather sad.*
MARK *is oblivious.*

LYDIA. Sebastian called. He's going to see it on a much better set than ours.

MARK. (*Doing it well.*) Oh really? Where?

JOEY. (*Eagerly.*) At his Editor's.

MARK. Well now, isn't that something! I wonder if Mr. Jeremy Thorpe is watching.

JOEY. Oh no.

MARK. Why not? One of his young hopefuls? Which is it going to be, Joey—writing or politics?

42

LYDIA. (*Firmly*.) Both. Now you sit here, Mark.

JOEY. No, I want you to sit there, and Mr. Walters here.

LYDIA. But this is more comfortable—

JOEY. I know. It's for you.

MARK. Ah, I get it. He wants his audience attentive.

LYDIA. Well, I'm his audience.

MARK. (*Sitting in the uncomfortable seat*.) You're his mother.

JOEY. (*From the set*.) Sh!

He turns the set's volume up.

ANNOUNCER. On B.B.C. 1, in thirty seconds time, there is Match of the Week—

JOEY. Of course that's what they'll all be watching.

LYDIA. Nonsense.

ANNOUNCER. (*Through this*.) Meanwhile on B.B.C. 2 there follows shortly a new thirty-minute play in the current series : Youth Theatre, entitled 'The Trial of Maxwell Henry Peabody', by Joseph Cruttwell.

There is music.

LYDIA. (*Sharply*.) *Joseph!* Why Joseph?

JOEY. It sounds more like a writer.

MARK. Yeah. It's a good name, Lydia. Joey's not too good. Joseph Cruttwell sounds like something—

JOEY. Thank you, Mr. Walters.

The music stops.

FIRST VOICE. (*Loudly*.) Maxwell Henry Peabody—come into court.

There is the sound of marching feet. LYDIA *and* MARK *are both forward in that attitude of strained attention natural to people watching a TV play under the observant scrutiny of the author, who has chosen a vantage point where he can see both screen and audience.*

The lights fade very quickly. There is a blackout for only a second before they come on again. LYDIA, MARK *and* JOEY *are in exactly the same strained attitudes as before. One might think no one has moved even a finger to scratch his or her nose.*

Have you anything to say why sentence should not be passed against you?

SECOND VOICE. But this is ridiculous. I have done nothing, I tell you—nothing, nothing, nothing—

FIRST VOICE. I agree. You have done nothing. Nothing to help your fellow human beings, nothing to save the world from the abyss into which it must soon finally fall, nothing save for your own material advantage—

SECOND VOICE. And my wife's. She's a director of several of my companies.

FIRST VOICE. And what did you do to save your son?

There is mocking laughter, followed by a blare of music, evidently signalling the end. Credits must follow because JOEY *kneels by the set, his nose practically touching it, to see his name go by.* LYDIA *crouches with him.*

LYDIA. There. Look how big his name is, Mark. Yes, Joseph is better.

She embraces him.

Darling, I'm so proud.

JOEY. (*Impatiently.*) But did you *like* it?

LYDIA. I loved it, Joey—

JOEY. (*Staring at her, puzzled.*) Did it make you cry?

LYDIA. A little. Wasn't it meant to?

JOEY. (*Doubtfully.*) Well it's really supposed to make one angry.

LYDIA. (*Reassuringly.*) Oh it did that too.

MARK. (*Choosing his words.*) Congratulations, young man, on a fine achievement—

The front door is unlocked. SEBASTIAN *appears, looking angry, holding in his hand* LYDIA'S *message which he has torn from the door.*

SEBASTIAN. What in hell's this? If after ten-thirty don't come in. I'm covering up—

He stops at sight of the television set in its prominent position, of LYDIA *in her smart dress, of* MARK *in a dinner jacket and of* JOEY *in one of his own shirts, all staring at him with varying expressions.*

Oh Christ—

JOEY *looks away from him first.*

JOEY. Good night, Mum. Thanks for watching.

LYDIA. But the champagne—

JOEY. No, thanks. Good night, Mr. Walters. Thanks for coming and for these

He indicates the cuff-links.

and for what you said.

MARK. It was good—real good, Joey. I mean it.

JOEY. Thanks.

In silence he walks up the stairs, hoping evidently to achieve dignity. But coming to the end he hurries his steps in a revealing way. LYDIA *looks after him.*

SEBASTIAN. Oh Lord—

LYDIA *suddenly swings one fist at him, and then the other. They are hard blows, with real fury behind them, and both connect.* SEBASTIAN, *off balance, and slightly unsteady anyhow, is knocked off his feet and falls, upsetting a table.*

LYDIA. (*With deep hatred.*) You bastard!

She turns and runs up the stairs after her son. SEBASTIAN *stays where he is, for a moment, putting his hand to his cheek, and shaking his head.* MARK *helps him to his feet.*

SEBASTIAN. (*Indicating television.*) Was it terrible?

MARK. Pretty terrible.

SEBASTIAN. (*In a chair.*) Get me a drink.

MARK. What is it? Scotch?

SEBASTIAN. (*Angrily.*) Of course Scotch.

With a deep sigh.

Oh, my God! I had it written down, I'd tied knots in everything, I'd remembered it at lunch—

He takes the drink from MARK.

And then after lunch something happened—

Pause. He stares into his glass.

A perfect excuse, I suppose, if I could use it. Perfect. But I can't.

MARK. What was it?

SEBASTIAN. I can't tell you either. Except—

He stares into his glass again.

I have to anyway—but not as an excuse.

Loudly.

I have no excuses. I am as God made me, which is an uncaring shit. Oh damn! Poor little bugger. She'd covered up for me?

MARK. You were watching it with your Editor.

SEBASTIAN. He's in Tangier.

MARK. The kid wouldn't have known that.

SEBASTIAN. Damn silly cover. I suppose it might have worked though. She'd have made it work. How has she been tonight— I mean apart from turning into Mohammed Ali?

MARK. Oh, fine, I thought.

SEBASTIAN. Fine, you thought. Did you look at all?

MARK. Sure. She didn't look too well, but I don't suppose she is, after her pass-out last night. Hungover, I'd say.

SEBASTIAN. Yes. Well, you'd better brace yourself, I suppose. Have you got a drink?

Mark holds his up

You're rather fond of this girl, aren't you?

MARK. I love her.

SEBASTIAN. And I suppose you're what might laughingly be called one of my best friends?

Finishing his drink.

Fill it up for me, would you?

MARK. Sure.

SEBASTIAN. Are you?

MARK. I think you are what you just said God made you, Sebastian—but maybe I'm not all that choosey about my best friends.

SEBASTIAN. Well I'm not either, or I wouldn't choose an ignorant, illiterate porn-monger—

MARK. (*Returning with the drink.*) O.K. O.K. I'm braced.

SEBASTIAN. That wasn't a pass-out last night—not an ordinary one. It was a small stroke.

Pause.

MARK. How do you know?

SEBASTIAN. She's had them before, and these last months they're getting more frequent. It's one of the things I've been told to look out for, you see—and it's one of the things you've got to look out for too when you take her away. I've got a list somewhere—

MARK. Surely the vodka—

SEBASTIAN. It probably helped—that and the cortisone—so don't let her wallow in the stuff as I did last night. She's been off any drink at all for over six months—so go fairly easy out there. Mind you the odd piss-up won't make much difference. Here's that list. Now I've got the doctor's address in Monte Carlo somewhere too—

He fumbles in his pockets again.

MARK. (*Quietly.*) Did you say cortisone?

SEBASTIAN. What? Yes. She's been on it six weeks. She doesn't know it, of course. Thinks they're iron pills, or something. Old Conny Ziegmann—he's her docor—'Uncle Constantin' she calls him—an ex-Estonian—he's quite a wonder. He can get her to

46

believe anything—where the hell did I put that address? Ah, here it is. Docteur Villoret. Address is on it.

MARK *takes it from him.*

Conny Ziegmann called him this afternoon, so he'll be wise to the situation, as your horrible phrase goes.

MARK. Could you, perhaps, put me wise too?

Pause. SEBASTIAN. *looks up at him.*

SEBASTIAN. I suppose so. I've been trying to put it off. I can't put it off any longer, can I?

Another pause.

She's in the terminal stages of leukemia.

Pause. SEBASTIAN *gets up and takes* MARK'S *glass to fill, patting his arm as he goes.*

Sorry. I had to tell you, you see, because old Conny Ziegmann wouldn't have let her go otherwise, unless I was along. I'm well-briefed, you see. What's that dreadful drink you have?

MARK. Bourbon. Did you say terminal?

SEBASTIAN. Yes.

MARK. How long does that mean?

SEBASTIAN. Three or four months. Six at most.

He hands MARK *the drink.*

MARK. Are you positive?

SEBASTIAN *laughs.*

SEBASTIAN. That's just the word, I'm afraid.

He pulls another paper from his pocket and hands it to MARK.

This cames from Conny Ziegmann by hand to the office this afternoon. He'd had it early this morning from the hospital, but couldn't call me because of Lydia. It's conclusive Lymphatic Leukemia.

MARK *stares at the paper with unseeing eyes. He knows, after all, its contents. Then he hands it back.*

Pause.

MARK. (*At length.*) So that's the something that happened to you after lunch.

SEBASTIAN. (*Distracted.*) What?—Yes. That. But I'd expected it. Conny hadn't given me any hope. He hasn't, really, for the last three months.

MARK. Who else has she seen?

SEBASTIAN. The best in the country. She doesn't know it, of course, but every man who looks her over in that hospital is hand-

47

picked. Of course they're casual with her, and don't give their names. But they've all been by courtesy of my kind Sunday paper—and all top boys on leukemia.

MARK. There are cures.

SEBASTIAN. Yes. There's this man in Denver, Colorado, who boasts a seventy per cent rate. But he's cagey. He won't take a case as advanced as this—

MARK. How do you know?

SEBASTIAN. I've asked him. I gave him all the facts and figures on the telephone, and got our medical correspondent to talk to him, too. No go, Mark. He won't risk that seventy per cent.

MARK. There's another man in Karlsruhe—

SEBASTIAN. I know about him too. He's just a phony. Christ, Mark, I haven't lacked for advice. If there'd been the faintest chance I'd have taken her to Timbuctoo—and told her I was covering Saharan Literature. I'd already got my story ready for Denver. I'd induced some wretched little local college to offer me a resident lectureship. Jesus, imagine that! . . . Now, Winnie Slobberwicz, stop groping your neighbour and listen. Balls-ache, as you are pleased to pronounce him, is the name of an important French writer and not an occupational disease —Oh, I'm sorry, Mark. My jokes are so feeble these days, it's a wonder she hasn't seen through them. And me. But she hasn't thank God. I mean, you've seen her alone. Does she have the faintest suspicion I'm concealing something from her.

MARK. No.

SEBASTIAN. Swear?

MARK. Swear.

SEBASTIAN. I'm good about never remembering when she's been to the doctor, getting his name wrong and never noticing when she's feeling ill. Also never on any account saying: 'Look I'll do that, darling. Don't you bother.' Can you imagine anything giving the show away quicker than that?

MARK. Frankly, I can't.

SEBASTIAN. Yes. Being one of Nature's shits does have its advantages when one's dealing with a dying wife.

He turns rather abruptly and goes into the hall. There he pulls down a hat box from the top of a bookcase where it has been visible throughout the play.

Say: 'Hullo Lydia' very loudly if you see her on the stairs.

He opens the hat-box and pulls out a lot of documents.

48

Copies of all her blood-counts, from six months ago. Conny sends them to me at the office every week. Can't keep them there. Too many nosey parkers.

He puts the latest missive on top of the others.

MARK. Can't you find a safer place than that?

SEBASTIAN. No. She goes round this flat prying into everything. Even the notes for my new novel which I carefully hid from her in my Gibbon's *Decline and Fall*—she got her nose into those yesterday.

He closes the lid and puts the hat-box back.

Dusting, she said. As if anyone would dust Gibbon without criminal intent—

MARK. A drawer with a lock?

SEBASTIAN. If I had one, she'd pick it. She'd never look up there.

He points to the replaced hat-box.

Clever, don't you think. I borrowed the idea from Edgar Alan Poe.

MARK. Mightn't she want to dust the hat?

SEBASTIAN. Don't be a clot. It was a topper to go to the Palace in for that O.B.E. thing and I gave it to Oxfam the next day. I keep the box there as an ornament. Anyway I've worked it out—neither she nor Mrs. MacHiggins can reach it. Clever, I think. I wasn't in Intelligence for nothing.

MARK. Sebastian, are you quite sure you shouldn't tell her?

SEBASTIAN. Quite sure. For six long years she had nothing to think of but dying. Now that she is I'm not letting her go through it again. And then if she had any inkling about it at all she'd worry herself sick over Joey—

MARK. Not over you?

SEBASTIAN. Over *me*? Why should she worry herself over me? She knows I can look after myself—

MARK. Does she?

SEBASTIAN. Well what with Mrs. MacHiggins and maybe Prunella—

MARK. You said yesterday—

SEBASTIAN. Yes. I laid that on pretty thick for her. Prunella's all right. She's no Lydia, but she's all right.

Pause.

No Lydia.

He begins to cry, fumbling for a handkerchief.

You've got to put up with this a bit, I'm afraid. Self-pity, of

49

course. You see the thing is, Mark, I didn't begin *really* to love her until I knew I was losing her.

MARK. That happens.

SEBASTIAN. Perhaps more to uncaring shits than to other people—like you, for instance. You've always loved her—

MARK. Yes.

SEBASTIAN. And I've—I've only had about six months. My fault, of course. Anybody but me would have started twenty-eight years earlier.

He hands out his drink to be refilled. MARK *takes it. Murmuring.*

No Lydia—
'She'll come no more.
Never, never, never, never never.'
Oh damn! I'll never review that bloody man again. I won't review anyone. After all they all make you blub somewhere—if they're good.

Angrily.

No, I'll write my own blub stuff—that's what I'll do—

MARK. Good idea.

SEBASTIAN. And *I'll* sell *ten* million paperbacks in advance—

MARK. *(Handing him his drink.)* Why not?

SEBASTIAN. Without one single power-mad tycoon. Just me—and her—changed, of course. The meeting in the whorehouse is far too melodramatic. But the same balance—gratitude and duty one side, taking for granted the other—the whole adding up to—something too late—and then—

He snaps his fingers. To MARK.

I suppose *you'll* have to be in it, as the escape she refused. Not as you are, of course. No one would believe that.

MARK. And Joey?

SEBASTIAN. Yes, Liberal Joey, I suppose. The new assenting young. Oh God, the poor little sod! He worships his mother. Too much, I suppose—but you can't blame him. Yes, he's going to be quite a handful after—

Pause.

I'll have to try. Tonight won't have helped much, will it?

MARK. You've got ten days.

SEBASTIAN. Ten days without her. I don't like to think of that much—

MARK. Then come too.

50

SEBASTIAN. No. I could—but I've got to get used to—try to get used to—oh damn! Did I feel about her like this from the beginning? It's possible. It's possible. And wouldn't allow myself to? Yes, possible.

Angrily.

Do you know what 'le vice Anglais?'—the English vice—really is? Not flagellation, not pederasty—whatever the French believe it to be. It's our refusal to admit to our emotions. We think they demean us, I suppose.

He covers his face.

Well I'm being punished now, all right—for a lifetime of vice. Very moral endings to a Victorian novel. I'm becoming maudlin. But, oh Mark, life without Lydia will be such endless misery.

He sees LYDIA *coming down the stairs.* SEBASTIAN *jumps up from his chair and turns his back, adroitly transforming emotion into huffiness.* LYDIA *looks at his back a long time. When* SEBASTIAN *turns to face her he is apparently dry-eyed, and holding his jaw as if in pain.*

SEBASTIAN. (*With dignity.*) Husband-beater!

LYDIA. I came to say I was sorry.

SEBASTIAN. I shall so inform my solicitors. Good night Mark.

MARK. Oh, am I going?

SEBASTIAN. No, I am.

He gives another withering glance at LYDIA, *rubs his cheek and walks towards his work-room, even contriving a limp as he does so.*

LYDIA. Are you going to work? Isn't it too late?

SEBASTIAN. Yes, to the first. No, to the second.

LYDIA. Wouldn't you like some of this food?

SEBASTIAN. It would turn to ashes in my mouth.

He goes out.

LYDIA. Did I hurt him?

MARK. Not enough.

LYDIA. I could have hit him much harder, you know. And kicked him too—on the ground. Queensbury Rules my fanny. Is he really working or just sulking?

MARK. Sulking, I'd say. I'm going.

LYDIA. (*Looking anxiously at* SEBASTIAN's *door.*) Yes, I suppose you'd better.

She kisses him.

Thank you so very much, Marcus. He really did appreciate it.

MARK. How is Joey?

LYDIA. He's bad, of course.

Angrily, at the door.

How could any human being do a thing like that to his son?

How *could* he? What's his excuse?

MARK. He forgot.

LYDIA. I mean his excuse for forgetting?

Pause.

MARK. About the best a man could have, I guess.

LYDIA. (*Amazed.*) You take his side.

MARK. Yes, on this.

LYDIA. Well what *is* his excuse?

MARK. Good night, Lydia.

He goes to the door, leaving LYDIA *looking bewildered. Turning.*

Oh Christ! Has anybody ever been in such a spot? Look—

He points to the hat-box.

That thing up there. It needs dusting.

LYDIA. The hat-box?

MARK. Yes. You can see the dust from here.

LYDIA. But I can't reach it.

MARK *points to some library steps.* LYDIA, *utterly bewildered, goes to get them.*

MARK. No. Not now. Tomorrow—when Sebastian's out. After you've dusted it—inside as well as out—you'll just have to play it your way—both of you. And then together or separately—tell me how *I'm* to play mine.

LYDIA. I see. He's hidden something there.

MARK. Yes.

LYDIA. Something he doesn't want me to see.

MARK. You bet.

LYDIA. The wily bastard. Love letters?

MARK. Kind of.

LYDIA. (*Aghast.*) You mean—serious?

MARK. Very serious, I think.

LYDIA. Larkin—I suppose—

MARK. No. Someone else.

LYDIA. Jesus—I wish I *had* kicked him. I wish I'd *killed* him.

Suddenly loyal.

52

And why are you giving him away? You're supposed to be his friend.

MARK. I'm supposed to be yours, too. That's what's made my life, these last two days, a little confusing. Call you tomorrow.

He goes out. LYDIA, *muttering imprecations, first looks at the hat-box, then firmly decides to resist the temptation. She comes into the sitting-room and sits down demurely. Then she looks at the hat-box again, and the library steps. Then she gets up cautiously and listens at* SEBASTIAN's *door. She hears him typing, and so do we. She darts to the library steps, rolls them into the hall and pulls down the hat-box, opening it and groping inside. Her fingers find what they are looking for and removes a pile of documents. Hastily she replaces the lid, and puts the hat-box back, leaving the library steps where they are. Then she puts on her glasses and settles herself on to the sofa for a belligerent, if furtive read.*

Three seconds later she has shot off the sofa. She riffles through the papers. They are all of identical size, and have needed no more than a few glances. They are, after all, familiar.

After a moment or two her legs give way, and she has to fall back on to the sofa. She has opened her bag to fumble for a handkerchief when SEBASTIAN *opens his door. It is the matter of a split second for an accomplished document-peeper to stuff the papers into her bag and close it. The budding tears are a different matter. She has to brush those away. And she is conscious too of the tell-tale library steps.*

SEBASTIAN. (*Gloomily.*) I've been trying to write him a letter you could shove under his door. But it's no good. My mandarin style gets in the way.

LYDIA. It would.

She gets up casually to drape herself somewhere near the hall, masking the library steps.

SEBASTIAN. I suppose I'd better see the little sod.

LYDIA. What little sod?

SEBASTIAN. Are there two in the flat? Where is he?

LYDIA. If you're referring to our son—Joseph Cruttwell, dramatist —he's in bed.

SEBASTIAN. Oh darling, do stop sniffling. You know how I hate it.

LYDIA. I wasn't sniffling.

SEBASTIAN. You were. I could hear you from in there.

53

A lie.
And those things under your eyes are tears, aren't they?
He peers from a distance.
I'm not coming in range. I think you should know I once hit
a sub-editor and he was off-duty for a week. And he wasn't
any smaller than you either. However, enough of that. About
Joey. What's done is done, and can by dint of my overwhelming
charm, be undone. I shall speak to him personally.
LYDIA. I shouldn't rely on your overwhelming charm.
SEBASTIAN. Thank you.
LYDIA. I mean why not just let him see you once as you really
are.
SEBASTIAN. I have no idea what that sibylline utterance is
supposed to mean. I think I know a father's duty towards his
son without prompting from you, Madam.
SEBASTIAN. Why are you leaning there like Isadora Duncan?
LYDIA. I've been putting books in their right places, under your
orders, sir.
SEBASTIAN. Good. That'll be a change. All right. Go and get the
little bugger down.
LYDIA. No.
SEBASTIAN. No?
LYDIA. You go up.
SEBASTIAN. (*Outraged.*) Go up? Knock timidly at his door and
beg leave to enter that room with all those Liberal Posters on
the wall—crawl across the carpet like a penitent, abase myself
like Henry IV at Canossa, scourge myself—all right, I'll go
up.
He goes to the stairs, climbing reluctantly.
Why are you looking at me like that?
LYDIA. A cat may look at a King.
SEBASTIAN. Are you pissed again?
LYDIA. Oh yes.
SEBASTIAN. Vodka.
LYDIA. Something—kind of—headier—
SEBASTIAN. Kirsch, or Slivovitz or something? My God, darling,
you'll end up in an alcoholics' ward.
He disappears. Immediately LYDIA *darts into the hall climbs the
steps and deposits the papers inside. She has just wheeled the
steps back when* SEBASTIAN *reappears.*
I looked in and the little bastard was asleep.

Relieved.

Tomorrow, don't you think?

He scoops some food on to a plate. Plying a fork.

Hm. This is rather good. Who made it? Joey?

LYDIA, *free now move, pulls her right fist back.*

Oh *you* did?

LYDIA. It's my crab mousse, and you've had it a million times.

SEBASTIAN. It just seemed better than usual.

JOEY, *in a dressing-gown, is coming downstairs. Both parents watch him as he walks in a dignified manner past his father, cutting him dead, and up to* LYDIA.

JOEY. I'm very sorry, Mum. I left you to clear up alone.

LYDIA. Oh that's all right, darling. I can do that myself.

JOEY. I'll help you.

He picks up two dishes and carries them up to the kitchen.

SEBASTIAN *exchanges a meaning glance with* LYDIA.

SEBASTIAN. (*Loudly.*) Darling would you fix that draught for me in there.

LYDIA. Oh, yes, I will.

JOEY *reappears, still walking with dignity.*

SEBASTIAN. I think it's coming from the window.

LYDIA. Yes. I shouldn't be surprised.

She goes into the work-room.

SEBASTIAN. Joey, put those things down.

JOEY, *at first, is inclined to disobey.* SEBASTIAN *takes them from him.*

Anyway I'm eating from this one.

JOEY. I'm very sorry. If I'd known I wouldn't have touched it.

SEBASTIAN. You've a perfect right to be as rude to me as you like, and to call me every name you can think of. Tonight I behaved to you as badly as any father has ever behaved to his son. If my father had done that to me when I was your age I'd have walked straight out of his house and never talked to him again.

JOEY. You did, didn't you?

SEBASTIAN. No. I was turned out. I may have told you I walked out, because it sounds better. In fact I was booted. A little trouble with one of the maids. I can only say, Joey, that tonight I behaved like a thoughtless bastard—that's the word your Mum used. To Mark I said 'shit'—'an uncaring shit' and meant it. I am that, sometimes, and I behave like

55

that sometimes. If you like you can say usually. Or even always. It may be true. But tonight was the worst thing I've ever done to anyone, anywhere. I may do some bad things to you, Joey, in the future—if we're still seeing each other—but one thing you must know—I can't ever do anything quite as bad as I did tonight. Not even I can break the world record of shittishness twice—

JOEY. I don't believe you forgot. I believe you did it deliberately.

SEBASTIAN. I can see you'd rather think that. So would I. It's less damaging to the ego. The plain, sordid fact is that I forgot.

JOEY. How could you, Dad?

SEBASTIAN. I did. And I have no excuse at all. Now listen. What I intend to do is this. I shall get our television man to ask to have it re-run—

JOEY. Oh Dad—this is all talk.

SEBASTIAN. At Television Centre, for me, for him—not for my Editor who's in Tangier—and for anyone else who wants to see it. You, of course, too. And our television critic will review it. I don't know what he'll say, and it'll have to be next week, but he'll mention it in his column, I promise.

JOEY. Is this on the level, or will you forget again?

SEBASTIAN. I said you could insult me, but there's no need to kick me in the crutch. Now if I do that for you will you do something for me?

JOEY. (*Suspiciously.*) What?

SEBASTIAN. Sit in that chair.

He forces him into one and then brings over the chess table.
And show me for once how you can justify all that hissing that goes on behind my chair.

JOEY. Dad, it's late.

SEBASTIAN. Only for Liberals. Not for men. Go on. You be white. Fifty pence on it?

JOEY. I'll want a two pawns' handicap.

SEBASTIAN. One.

JOEY. Done.

SEBASTIAN *takes one of his pawns off.* JOEY *moves.* SEBASTIAN *moves.* JOEY *moves.*

SEBASTIAN. That's not in *my* 'Twelve Easy Openings for Beginners'.

SEBASTIAN *moves.* JOEY *thinks.* LYDIA, *who has plainly had her*

56

ear glued to the keyhole slips out of the work-room. She watches them for a second. JOEY *moves.* SEBASTIAN *moves.*

JOEY. (*Rising.*) Right. My game.

SEBASTIAN. What do you mean your game?

JOEY. You moved your King three squares.

SEBASTIAN. I beg your pardon, my Queen.

Horrified.

My *King?* Oh blast and bugger that Mark Walters! These pieces are going straight back to Hong-Kong. I told him a hundred times—

He is putting the pieces back on the board again. JOEY *has stood up.*

JOEY. Fifty pence, please.

SEBASTIAN. Are you mad, boy?

JOEY. The rules say firmly—

LYDIA. You must play the rules, dear.

SEBASTIAN. You keep out of this! Go and do something useful somewhere. Better still, go to bed.

JOEY. Yes, Mum. We'll clear up.

SEBASTIAN. Yes, Joey will clear up.

LYDIA. Give Joey his fifty pence.

SEBASTIAN. Oh bugger you both!

He forks up.

LYDIA. Charming loser, isn't he?

SEBASTIAN. Loser my arse! I didn't lose. I made a tiny human error in lying out these monstrosities of chessmen—

JOEY *is going.* SEBASTIAN *catches his sleeve.*

Oh, my boy. Oh no. If you think you're taking that fifty pence of mine to bed, you're making a big mistake. All right. Start again. Double or quits. Same moves, but this time with the right pieces in the right places—

They move rapidly, in silence. LYDIA *watches them for a moment, putting her arm lightly on* SEBASTIAN's *shoulder.*

LYDIA. Well, good night.

JOEY *jumps up to kiss his mother.*

SEBASTIAN. (*Irritated.*) Don't do that. It upsets concentration. You could have kissed her sitting down, couldn't you?

He does exactly that, slapping her playfully on the behind. She goes to the stairs. SEBASTIAN *concentrates on the board. To* JOEY.

I'm afraid your Jeremy Thorpe is coming under a little pressure.

E 57

JOEY. Your Mao Tse Tung doesn't look too happy either, Dad.
LYDIA *turns to look back at them.*
SEBASTIAN. *(To* JOEY.) Yes, I can see you have played before.
Well, well, well. Do you know those ten days without her might
be quite fun—
*He looks up casually. If we didn't know his secret we might
even believe him when he says:*
Oh sorry, darling. Didn't see you were still there.
LYDIA *smiles. In fact, radiantly.*
LYDIA. I know you didn't.
SEBASTIAN. Go on. Move, Joey.
She goes on slowly up the stairs.
We haven't got all night ahead of us.
LYDIA *disappears from sight.*
Except, I suppose, we have.

CURTAIN

58

BEFORE DAWN

Characters
THE BARON
THE LACKEY
THE CAPTAIN
THE DIVA

Setting: Rome
Time: The Early Hours of June 17, 1800

A room in the Castel Sant' Angelo. One door is visible (R) which leads—we will discover—to a bedroom. Steps lead up to it. Another door (L) is invisible but extremely audible, as it invariably opens (off) with a loud clanging of bolts and bars. There is a window at the back. The essential furniture is a desk (L), a settee and armchairs placed wherever convenient. Also, in a corner, a prie-dieu, with an image of the Virgin, lit by a lamp.

Most prominent of all is a supper table, covered with a cloth, on which is a fairly lavish cold collation, with two or three bottles of wine. A MAN sits at it, served by a LACKEY. The table is lit by candelabra, and so is the desk, but outside these two circles of light the room is shadowy and sinister.

In short, if the set bears a strong resemblance to Act IV of Sardou's TOSCA, (or to Act II of the opera of the same name) it should not too much surprise us: for the gentleman now gorging himself at the supper table is called the BARON SCARPIA and he is the Regent of Police to the Bourbons of Naples whose troops, after driving out the French Revolutionary armies and destroying the short-lived 'People's Roman Republic', are currently occupying Rome, until the arrival of the new Pope Pius VII, recently elected in Austrian-occupied Venice. And BARON SCARPIA is, of course, a very famous villain indeed, the prototype of all the nineteenth century moustache-twirlers and 'proud-beauty trappers' to come. He is being served by a liveried LACKEY.

SCARPIA. What is the time?
Even as he speaks he is answered by the thunder of metal on metal.
    The room must be very close to the clock tower, if not in it. There are two echoing peals before the LACKEY can reply.
LACKEY. Two, your Excellency.
SCARPIA. (*Crossly.*) I know, now. Open that window. The air is stifling.
The LACKEY does so. Other clocks, more distant, are striking all over Rome.
(*Angrily.*) And now I can smell the Tiber drains—
The LACKEY moves to close the window.
    No.
The LACKEY leaves the window open.
    SCARPIA *finishes his plate and takes a gulp of wine, followed by a pinch of snuff.*

61

The horror of these apartments! If His Sicilian Majesty only knew the conditions under which I slave for him—

LACKEY. He'd make you a Duke at the least, Excellency.

SCARPIA. Duca di Scarpia? The sound is not right. Baron is more frightening; and in my post you have to be frightening or nothing.

LACKEY. His Excellency is not nothing.

SCARPIA. Thank you, Giuseppe. No, it's not a Dukedom I want. It's more money.

There is a loud knock at the unseen iron door. SCARPIA *makes a gesture to the* LACKEY *to open it. While he goes to do so,* SCARPIA *pours himself a glass of wine—red this time—from another bottle. There is a clatter of bolts and bars and* SCHIARRONE *comes in. He is in the uniform of a Captain of the Guard, and is a rather breathless young man, easily confused.*

You may leave us, Giuseppe.

GIUSEPPE *bows low and disappears. Again we hear the clanging of the iron door.*

SCHIARRONE. I have doubled the guards all over the city, Excellency, and I have put the whole garrison on instant alert.

SCARPIA. (*Sipping wine.*) I wonder if that was necessary. Everything seems very calm.

SCHIARRONE. Everything is not always what it seems, Excellency.

SCARPIA. (*Eyeing him with disfavour.*) True. Very true. Tell me Schiarrone, how did you get yourself promoted Captain so very young?

SCHIARRONE. The fates have been kind, Excellency.

SCARPIA. So, I would imagine, has someone else.

SCHIARRONE. Your Excellency is pleased to mock my aristocratic connections?

SCARPIA. Oh no. I never mock any connections, aristocratic or popular. You fancy the city to be on the verge of a violent revolution?

SCHIARRONE. When news of the northern battle reaches the people—

SCARPIA. The news won't reach them for two days—and then only in the form in which I choose to give it.

SCHIARRONE. Even your Excellency's well-known skill at doctoring disasters to sound like triumphs can hardly conceal from them the fact that there is nothing now between Bonaparte and Rome—

SCARPIA. Two hundred leagues are not nothing, Schiarrone.

SCHIARRONE. I meant no forces. General Melas' surrender at Marengo—

SCARPIA. You mean there are no Austrian forces. But why do you ignore our own skilled and determined Neapolitan armies?

SCHIARRONE. Excellency, I am an ardent admirer of our southern countrymen and no one is more alive to Sicilian and Neapolitan virtues than I—a simple Roman—

SCARPIA. But you would not put martial ardour very high on the list?

SCHIARRONE. Forgive me, Excellency.

SCARPIA. There is nothing to forgive. I said our armies were skilled and determined. I did not say what they were skilled and determined at. So far in these wars it has been pillaging, looting, raping and running.

SCHIARRONE. (*Helplessly.*) So what *can* stop Bonaparte from taking Rome?

SCARPIA. Let us put our faith in God. As a Cardinal's son I presume you believe in Him.

SCHIARRONE. (*Scandalised.*) Excellency! Oh, Excellency!

SCARPIA. Oh dear! I'm so sorry. Nephew of course. But then he treats you just like a son?

SCHIARRONE *nods.*

Well you must get your—uncle to say a very powerful Mass or two in the next few days.

Tranquilly he pours out another glass, offering the bottle to SCHIARRONE, *who shakes his head.*

With these high connections of which you boast, how did you escape guillotining during our late Roman Republic?

SCHIARRONE. It's a long story.

SCARPIA. Tell it.

SCHIARRONE. My mother, who was a dancer, used to know the president of the Revolutionary Tribunal—

SCARPIA. But that's a very short story.

SCHIARRONE. There's much more to tell—

SCARPIA. Not very much, surely? Connections both aristocratic and popular? Well you seem well armoured against almost any eventuality in these troubled times—except possibly an invasion by the Americans. Excellent wine.

63

Getting up from the table.
Well, how is our prisoner? Attending reverently, I trust, to his last moments on earth?

SCHIARRONE. He is in the Chapel with the White Friars of Death. But he has deeply distressed those holy men by refusing to recognise their Order, by denying the right of His Sicilian Majesty to have him executed without trial, and by claiming that he has committed no offence against the people of Rome, but only against their oppressors. The time, he says, is at hand when the sacred ideals of Liberty, Equality and Fraternity—
He is stopped by a gesture from SCARPIA.

SCARPIA. Yes, yes. Well fraternity he now has, liberty he soon will have, and everyone is equal in death.
He chuckles villainously.
Tell me, was he surprised that we knew his plans so well?

SCHIARRONE. Yes, Excellency. He has been perfectly honest about that. His rising was carefully timed for the eve of Bonaparte's entry into the Papal States, and his orders came directly, via the French agents who are everywhere in Rome, from Fouché himself.

SCARPIA. *(Absently.)* From Fouché?

SCHIARRONE. Yes, Excellency. The head of Bonaparte's secret police—

SCARPIA. *(Interrupting with a bellow.)* Idiot! Do you think I am unaware of who Fouché is? What kind of a secret police-man would *I* make if I didn't know the name of my counter-part in Paris?
With an undisguised note of respect.
Indeed the acknowledged head of my profession, Schiarrone. He may well be the best, most terrible and most efficient chief of Secret Police who has ever lived, anywhere, at any time. It is a poor general who does not respect his opponent. So Signor Cavaradossi has no idea at all how I found out all the details of his insurrection?

SCHIARRONE. He knows that somehow you infiltrated his group and that one of his fellow-conspirators is a traitor, but he has no idea which. Just for me, Excellency—in confidence—which one is it?

SCARPIA. The last to be shot, of course. Use your wits, Schiarrone. Well, use something anyway. Cavaradossi goes first, of course. How long is it to dawn?

SCHIARRONE. Under two hours—

SCARPIA. Where is the lady?

SCHIARRONE. In the room your Excellency ordered her to be locked in.

SCARPIA. Has it windows?

SCHIARRONE. A skylight—barred.

SCARPIA. Good. These opera singers can be temperamental, and —well—her suicide would be unfortunate. The Queen adores her, for some reason.

SCHIARRONE. No doubt because she sings so exquisitely.

SCARPIA. Well the Queen also adores Lady Hamilton, who doesn't. There may be some other reason, beyond masculine ken, Schiarrone, and certainly beyond mine as Her Majesty's loyal subject and her husband's Regent of Police. Well, you can bring her in.

As SCHIARRONE *salutes to leave.*

Oh, Schiarrone, one most important thing. Goodness I nearly forgot!

While eating.

Now at some stage in my conversation with the lady I may have occasion to summon you back to give you some perfectly idiotic instructions.

SCHIARRONE. In what way idiotic, Excellency?

SCARPIA. (*Sharply.*) In that they are on no account to be obeyed. I may, for instance, tell you to disarm the firing party and re-arm them with blank ammunition, for Cavaradossi to be warned to feign dead at the fatal volley, and then some nonsense about smuggling him off in a coach with drawn blinds to Milan, or somewhere—

SCHIARRONE. (*Armed with notebook and pencil.*) Er—could I have this in writing, Excellency? It seems a little complicated—

SCARPIA. It is not in the least complicated. Your orders are simple. They are to disobey any orders that I give you in the hearing of the lady. Just that and nothing more.

Pause.

SCHIARRONE. Supposing you order me to carry out my first orders?

SCARPIA. (*Impatiently.*) Then you carry out your first orders.

SCHIARRONE. Ah, but that wouldn't be *disobeying* your orders, would it? Please, Excellency, I really think it would be better in writing—

SCARPIA. I can't give it to you in writing, idiot. I don't know the lady's mind yet.

SCHIARRONE. Ah. I begin to see.

SCARPIA. (*Muttering.*) God in heaven!

SCHIARRONE. (*Brightly.*) It would perhaps avoid all confusion if your Excellency, when giving me an order that is to be disobeyed, could manage to give me a little wink?

SCARPIA. (*Spluttering.*) Yes. That would look very convincing, wouldn't it? 'Tell the firing party to disarm their muskets and reload with blanks—'

He gives a large, operatic wink.

SCHIARRONE. But please Excellency—*some* sign. This is plainly a very delicate matter. It seems to concern a lady's honour—also, of course, a man's life. Your Excellency would not wish me to make an utter—fiasco of it. Perhaps a handkerchief dropped —something like that.

SCARPIA. All right. A handkerchief dropped. I shall make my meaning plain, never fear. Fetch the lady!

SCHIARRONE *goes.* SCARPIA *sips. A* clock—the *clock*—thunderously *strikes the quarter.* SCARPIA, *looking pleased both with himself and the world, smiles and nods, before finishing his glass of wine. There is a great clattering of bolts and bars and suddenly* LA TOSCA *is standing just inside the room, half in shadow.* SCARPIA *rises slowly. He bows politely. She makes no sign.*

You will want to know where you are, Tosca. You are in the Castel Sant' Angelo. You were brought here secretly with a hood over your face, after my police had arrested Signor Mario Cavaradossi in your cellars. Oh what a stupid hiding-place, Signora! A wanted terrorist with a price on his head, to take refuge in the house of a lady whom all Rome knows he loves. What is more, a lady whose revolutionary sympathies are not exactly unknown to the authorities. Did you not once before have a little trouble with my police for singing the Marseillaise in Italian from the top of the Spanish Steps?

TOSCA. (*In a low voice.*) Where is Mario?

SCARPIA. Now, do you know that I have never heard the Marseillaise sung in Italian? To hear it sung by you must be a sublime experience. You would not, I suppose, care to sing it for me now?

TOSCA (*As before.*) Where is Mario? I demand to ask!

SCARPIA. I hardly think that you are in a position to demand anything, Signora. To harbour a known criminal is itself a crime.

TOSCA. He is not a criminal, and nor am I.

SCARPIA. Well, there might be different opinions on that. By the way would you care for a little wine?

TOSCA *makes a scornful gesture of refusal.*

It's excellent, you know. Genuine French—and a good revolutionary vintage—1792. Does not even the year tempt you?

She makes another scornful gesture. SCARPIA *begins to move about. She remains still.*

Pity. Well I suppose a good lawyer might plead on your behalf that you, being an artist, an opera singer and a dreamer, might have been totally unaware of your lover's plan to overthrow the State—

TOSCA. (*Scornfully.*) Overthrow the State? And who says that *that* is a crime?

SCARPIA. Well, oddly enough, the State.

TOSCA. The State? *This* State?—Bah!

Pause.

SCARPIA. Do you know that would sound very well sung. Music by—who do you think? Haydn—Mozart—?

TOSCA. Where is Mario?

SCARPIA. He is very close to you indeed—just beyond that wall there—

Pointing to wall L.

in the Chapel of the White Friars of Death.

TOSCA.—of Death?

SCARPIA. I fear so, yes. He is due to die in two hours. Here is the warrant for his execution at dawn—today.

He takes out a document from his pocket, flourishes it briefly and replaces it quickly.

The news must of course distress you very much. I had hoped to spare you knowledge of it—but then you were so very insistent.

TOSCA. To—die—without even a trial?

Hitting the desk hard with both hands.

Oh monstrous! Monstrous! Monstrous! Oh cruel! Unspeakable!

SCARPIA. (*Interrupting rather tetchily.*) Signora, do please stop doing that, or you'll do yourself an injury.

He pulls her away from the desk.

Or the desk one.

He examines the top.

It is an exquisite piece. Believe it or not, it belonged to the Borgias—

TOSCA. Ah I believe it! To the Borgias, yes! That is what Rome has become now again under these Neapolitan assassins! To execute a man without hearing him speak? Ah, Monstrous!

SCARPIA. Oh, we've heard him speak. At great length, in fact, and without interrupting him once, although every word he uttered was either treason, or blasphemy, or both. And in the course of his eloquence he has freely confessed to everything of which he stands accused.

TOSCA. Who signed that warrant?

SCARPIA. The man under whose orders I work, and whose orders I must obey.

TOSCA. The Military Governor? The Queen will countermand it—

SCARPIA. Yes. No doubt she would have if we had allowed you access to her tonight—

TOSCA. Fiend! Was it for that reason that I have been kept here in that locked room all these hours?

SCARPIA. Oh, not officially. Officially you were brought here to help us in our enquiries. It was, after all, in your house that we discovered the cuprit. But you may take it from me, my dearest Diva, that our enquiries are now ended, and you are perfectly free to go.

Pause.

TOSCA (*Puzzled.*) Then I *will* go. Have your servants find me a carriage.

SCARPIA. Our clemency hardly extends to a carriage. If you go now you will have to walk or run.

TOSCA *hesitates,* SCARPIA *laughs.*

Exactly. If you cover the distances required as fast as that runner from Marathon—and you are surely capable of that feat—I fear that you will arrive back here, gasping and panting and flourishing the Queen's reprieve, at least an hour too late—

The clock strikes the half hour—and a quarter.

TOSCA. Villain! Perfidious murderer! The Queen will have you hanged for this!

SCARPIA. I rather doubt if the sister of Marie-Antoinette will hang the executioner of a would-be regicide.

TOSCA. Assassin! Oh brutal and most bloody tiger! Ten times accursed fiend!

SCARPIA. Oh Signora, please stop! You really mustn't blame *me*, but the man who signed this warrant.

Tapping his breast pocket.

I merely obey his orders. I deplore them, of course, but I must obey them—or else—

He makes the gesture of his own throat being cut.

TOSCA. A hypocrite too, as well as all else! Ah God—Without a trial—oh, it is too hard! Too hard!

SCARPIA. Deplorable, as I've agreed. But then, dear Tosca, were *your* friends in the late Roman Revolutionary Republic always so nice about giving *their* victims a trial?

TOSCA. (*Still indignant.*) But they were our enemies. They were trying to overthrow the State—

SCARPIA *smiles mildly at her, allowing her to grasp the inadequacy of her argument, before gently approaching her.*

SCARPIA. You see. It all depends on what is the State, and who are its enemies. In moral terms there is really nothing to choose between us—

TOSCA. Most certainly there is. We are on the side of Liberty, and you are against it. Tyrants, villains, assassins, brutal oppressors of the people—!

SCARPIA. (*Stopping her, this time with authority.*) No, not another aria, please. Believe me the cause of Liberty is not worth it.

TOSCA. Don't speak of sacred Liberty! Your lips sully its name.

SCARPIA. I simply ask myself the question: Will the French be more free under a First Consul than under a King?

TOSCA. Of course they will. Bonaparte is the greatest man who ever lived. He is the personification of the invincible power of World Revolution.

SCARPIA. Is he? Well, I agree that at this precise moment of history he hardly seems very vincible.

TOSCA (*Eagerly.*) You have news of the battle in the north?

SCARPIA. I fear I have. It would appear that our forces have met with a slight reverse at the village of Marengo—

TOSCA. (*With the full force of her lungs.*) Vittoria! Vittoria!

69

Those familiar with the opera will know that this famous cry from Act II is sung unaccompanied, in a triumphant crescendo by MARIO *from offstage.* TOSCA's *version is perhaps less musical —for she has not yet had the chance of hearing Puccini's opera —but it is loud and full-toned.*

SCARPIA. (*Alarmed.*) I beg your pardon—Oh, I'm so sorry. You were improvising—

TOSCA. My hero has not failed me. Ah, great Bonaparte! Liberty, Equality, Fraternity—You will conquer the world. Little reactionary pig, you have had your day! Turn now and salute the new dawn—before you bow your tyrant's head to its inevitable fate!

She is pointing to a sky that is still pitch black.

SCARPIA. The only thing is, Tosca, that this particular dawn, when it comes, is the last thing that you should salute, because it isn't my fate that it looks likely to bring, but someone else's. Well, to business. Now, Signora Tosca, this is the situation. Deeply as I regret this little matter about your lover, Mario Cavaradossi, my orders regarding it are formal and absolute. They can only be disobeyed at the greatest possible risk to my own life. Now that is not a risk that I would ordinarily be expected to take, nor would I think of it, were not you, Tosca, Rome's adored one—and my own adored one—so intimately involved. Do sit down now, take a glass of wine, and discuss with me sensibly, how the two of us can possibly manage to rescue Signor Cavaradossi from his deplorable predicament. Because there must *be* a way. There simply must. And your idol, the First Consul, is too far away from Rome to solve it for us.

He pours two glasses of wine, not looking at her.

TOSCA *suddenly strides to the table, and sits down with her right arm outstretched and her left hand clutching a wine glass. She contrives, in doing so, to look very like Sarah Bernhardt, in the famous photograph.*

TOSCA. How much?

Pause.

SCARPIA. I beg your pardon?

TOSCA. What is your price?

SCARPIA. Oh I see, my price? The highest, Tosca, that you can pay.

TOSCA. Name it. There is no price too high for Mario's life.

70

SCARPIA. None?

TOSCA. You can have my house, my jewels, my savings, my furs, my Persian rugs—

SCARPIA. Ha!

TOSCA. Why do you laugh? My Persian rugs are worth a fortune. I collect them and have been well-advised—

SCARPIA. Ha!

TOSCA. What *is* your price?

SCARPIA. You.

TOSCA. What?

SCARPIA. (*Rising.*) The price is you, Tosca, and I shall have my price.

He attempts to embrace her, but she is a muscular lady and she repels him without difficulty.

TOSCA. (*Laughing.*) Imbecile! I would rather jump through that window!

In the struggle, brief though it has been, SCARPIA *has been a trifle winded. It is a little time before he can manage to regain himself sufficiently to deliver the following—also immortal—line with the requisite dignity.*

SCARPIA. Jump then! Your lover follows you! I wonder how it will please Signor Cavaradossi to see your shattered body lying there in the courtyard. It will be the last sight of anything in this world that he will have before they put the blindfold over his eyes, and shoot their lead balls into his heart—

Gasping just a little, he is forced to swallow his glass of wine, with a rather trembling hand.

TOSCA. Oh, Monster! What is this vile bargain you propose?

Pause. SCARPIA, *his calm regained, pours another glass.*

SCARPIA. Really, Signora, the matter is perfectly simple. Say the word yes, and I save your lover. Say the word no, and I kill him. Now I can hardly make myself clearer than that, can I?

Pause. TOSCA *gathers a deep, operatic breath.*

TOSCA. Lecherous wretch!—devil incarnate!—brutish beast!— fiend from hell!—lustful spawn of Satan—

SCARPIA. Yes, yes, I know all that, but what we have to decide, fairly soon, is whether—

TOSCA *has not filled her lungs for nothing. She sails straight through him.*

TOSCA. Pig! Monster! Degenerate jackal! From what womb were you ripped? No human one, that's certain. No woman

71

born of man could have suckled such a satyr, nurtured in the noisome swamps of evil, weened in the wilderness of Satan—

SCARPIA. Oh do stop, Tosca! Time, you know, is running out. Now which is it to be? Yes—or no? A simple question surely deserves a simple answer.

Pause. She draws more breath.

TOSCA. I shall call from that window and proclaim your infamy to the whole of Rome.

SCARPIA. Even with your magnificent lungs no one will hear you. And if they did my infamy would hardly be news. Now, yes or no. Which is it to be?

TOSCA. I would rather defile myself with a leper.

SCARPIA. (*Nodding.*) Well, I think we might call that a fairly definitive no.

He goes to pull the bell-cord.

TOSCA. (*Suddenly human and pathetic.*) No.

SCARPIA. (*His hand still on the bell-cord.*) Do you mean no, no, or no, yes?

TOSCA. What pleasure can it give you to take to your bed a woman who must hate you will all her heart, despise you will all her mind, and resist you with all her body?

Pause.

SCARPIA. A good question.

He drops his hand from the bell-cord.

Well, I suppose the answer is this. I don't flatter myself that I am a particularly attractive man, Tosca, but you'd really be surprised how easy it has always been for me to entice women—desirable women too—into my bed. And they come there willingly. Nearly always too willingly. A Chief of Police is rather a marked man in that respect. Of course sometimes he is asked for little favours—a lover released, a husband condemned, a peccadillo of their own overlooked. But a very surprising proportion of them want no favours at all. They find my position rather glamorous, you see, and like to boast afterwards of having been ravished by the brutal Chief of Police in his lair at the Castel Sant'Angelo. But really, you know, it's nearly always I who have been the one to be ravished.

With a sigh.

That becomes irksome, you know—

TOSCA. (*A half lung-full.*) Cynical rogue! Decadent lackey of the bourgeoisie! How I loathe your vile boasting—

SCARPIA. (*Excitedly.*) Ah. Now you see—that's just the point. You do loathe me, honestly and genuinely, and if you could only bring yourself to accompany me in there—

He points to door R.

you will loathe me even more, perhaps biting me and scratching me and even spitting in my face—

He is approaching her slowly.

and shouting out your insults, until suddenly your outraged body ceases to struggle and begins to tremble as it slowly— oh so slowly—becomes part of my own trembling body—and then suddenly, as the climax comes to both of us, your flesh is slave to my flesh, and your pleasure becomes my joy. Your hate and my desire will be a coupling for the gods! Oh Tosca, endure your torture, and give me my bliss!

He is staring at her from very close. But he does not try to embrace her. In that respect he has learnt his lesson.

TOSCA. Never! Never in this life!

SCARPIA. (*Pulls the bell-cord.*) A pity.

SCHIARRONE *comes in.*

SCHIARRONE. (*Breathlessly.*) Your Excellency's orders?

SCARPIA. You know them.

SCHIARRONE. Do I?

SCARPIA. (*Savagely.*) Carry out the execution.

TOSCA *goes rigid. But so too does* SCHIARRONE.

SCHIARRONE. That means—?

TOSCA. (*Throwing herself at* SCARPIA's *feet.*) No, no, no! Have pity! Have mercy! See I am at your feet, as a beggar before a King. Is that not enough for you?

SCARPIA. No.

To SCHIARRONE.

Carry it out.

As SCHIARRONE's *puzzled face grows more puzzled.*

Well, what are you waiting for?

SCHIARRONE. Has your Excellency, by any chance, dropped something?

SCARPIA. What?

He follows SCHIARRONE's *stare around his feet.*

No, idiot! Your *first* orders. Carry them out!

SCHIARRONE *quickly refers to his notebook. His face clears.*

SCHIARRONE. Yes, Excellency. As your Excellency *first* ordered.

He turns.

TOSCA. No, wait.

SCHIARRONE *turns to* SCARPIA *for confirmation.*

SCARPIA. Yes, wait.

SCHIARRONE *promptly marches towards the door. Shouting:*
I said 'wait' fool!

SCHIARRONE. (*Muttering.*) Oh, it's so confusing.

SCARPIA. Speak, Tosca.

SCHIARRONE *has waited.* TOSCA *having noticed nothing, has picked herself up gracefully from* SCARPIA's *feet. She is going to make the most of her next line, and takes her time in arranging to do so. She even fills her lungs, although the line will hardly demand it.*

TOSCA. (*To* SCARPIA, *in a despairing murmur.*) Yes.

SCARPIA. Schiarrone, I have changed my mind. I have further orders for you.

SCHIARRONE. (*Murmuring.*) Oh heavens!
He takes out his notebook again.
Yes, Excellency?

SCARPIA. You will not shoot Signor Mario Caravadossi.

SCHIARRONE. (*Obediently.*) Not shoot—
He looks around at SCARPIA's *feet again.*

SCARPIA *understands and begins to feel for a handkerchief.* TOSCA, *happily for both of them, has covered her face with her hands and is silently weeping.*

SCARPIA. That is correct. Now, I'll tell you what you are to do. (*His search has been unavailing.*) You are to fake the execution—

SCHIARRONE. (*Taking it down but still looking for the handkerchief.*) Fake the execution—

SCARPIA. You will order the firing party to remove the live ammunition from the muskets—

SCHIARRONE. (*Still looking for the signal.*) Live ammunition from their muskets—

SCARPIA. And replace them with—Schiarrone, do you happen to have a handkerchief on you?

SCHIARRONE. No, Excellency.

SCARPIA. (*Laughing hollowly.*) Funny—neither of us with a handkerchief!

SCHIARRONE. (*Suspiciously.*) Very funny, Excellency.

TOSCA. (*With a wail.*) Oh, what have I said?

SCARPIA. You've said 'yes', dear.

To SCHIARRONE.

I think I must have *dropped* my handkerchief somewhere.

SCHIARRONE. Ah. And if I *had* had one and *had* lent it to your Excellency then your Excellency might well have *dropped* that too?

SCARPIA. We understand each other. Splendid fellow!

SCHIARRONE. *(Bowing, delighted.)* Excellency!

TOSCA. *(From wherever she has been weeping.)* How are you going to save my Mario?

SCARPIA. Well, if you listen you will hear. I have an ingenious plan.

He nods affably to SCHIARRONE *to continue his writing, but* SCHIARRONE *has put his notebook away.*

Quite right, Schiarrone. These things are better not written down.

Of course SCHIARRONE *has brought his notebook out again.*

Very well. For your own security. The live ammunition is to be removed from the firing-party's muskets, and in their place you will serve them only with powder.

SCHIARRONE. *(Writing vigorously.)* Gun powder?

SCARPIA. *(With a look.)* Gun powder. Now you will warn Signor Cavaradossi that when he hears the volley he must fall to the ground, and appear to be dead. You are then to approach the body—

TOSCA. *(Caught lungless but making a good show.)* Ah—

SCARPIA. *(When he can.)*—of the *live* Signor Cavaradossi, announce him to be dead—or give him a fake coup de grace—whichever you prefer—

SCHIARRONE. As the inspiration takes me, Excellency? I mean things like coups de grace can't really be arranged in advance, can they? It so much depends, doesn't it?

Looking up and getting SCARPIA'*s steely glance.*

I mean, even in a *fake* execution.

SCARPIA. Even in a *fake* execution.

SCHIARRONE. Yes, Excellency.

Hesitantly.

I still have your meaning, I think.

SCARPIA. I hope so. Now a coach with drawn blinds will be waiting in the courtyard. When the firing party is dismissed you will take Cavaradossi into it , and escort him past the Porta Angelica, using my name and authority. You will give orders for the coach to drive directly to Milan, and arrange suitable changes of horses. Before that , I will have some orders for you regarding a carriage to take Signora Tosca to her home.

SCHIARRONE. When will that be, Excellency?

SCARPIA. Some time before dawn.

SCHIARRONE. Could you be more precise?

SCARPIA. (*Angrily.*) No, I could not.

SCHIARRONE. (*Whispering.*) Oh, I see. When you have taken your pleasure—

SCARPIA. (*Loudly.*) Exactly. Now is all that understood, Schiarrone?

SCHIARRONE. (*Fervently.*) Oh God, I hope so.

SCARPIA. Leave us.

SCHIARRONE *begins to go and then turns in doubt. A furious gesture from* SCARPIA *sends him flying. Bolts and bars rattle again and then there is silence.* TOSCA *is at the window, her back to* SCARPIA. *He approaches her and puts his arm on her shoulder. She shrinks away.* SCARPIA *laughs, with relish.*

My dearest Diva, have I organised it well enough for you?

TOSCA. There is one more thing—

SCARPIA. Yes?

TOSCA. I will want to visit my beloved in Milan.

SCARPIA. Of course you will. Very well. I will write you the necessary document.

He sits down, his back to her and begins to write.

TOSCA *very warily approaches the table, prominent on which is a large bread-knife. She takes it up.*

SCARPIA *turns almost at the same moment and* TOSCA *conceals the knife, with a lightning gesture, behind her back.*

Lucky Milan! Now the Scala will have a chance to hear that magnificent organ of yours.

TOSCA. (*Icily.*) You are too kind, Baron.

He turns to write again. With a bound TOSCA *is on him, stabbing him in the back with all her might. As she strikes:*

Villain! Bloody, bawdy villain! Remorseless, lecherous, treacherous, kindless villain! Ah, vengeance!

The knife is driven remorselessly into SCARPIA'S *back, but seems to have no effect whatever. After he has received about five full-bodied blows,* SCARPIA *gets up and politely hands* TOSCA *a document.*

SCARPIA. Your laisser-passer, Signora. *He removes his tunic to*

76

reveal a leather under-garment reminiscent of a bullet-proof jacket. He studies the tunic carefully.) This will have to go to the tailor's. The last two ladies hardly scratched the fabric. I congratulate you, Signora, on the power of your thrust.

SCARPIA *takes off his leather vest; then with perfect politeness, opens the door to the bedroom inviting her, with a gesture, inside. Pause* TOSCA *drops a quick reverence to the Virgin before going to the door.*

(*Smiling.*) I thought, as a good revolutionary, you only believed in the Goddess of Reason?

TOSCA. How can the Goddess of Reason help me now?

She goes past him into the room.

SCARPIA. (*Sympathetically.*) I See Your Point.

He follows her off.

As the lights begin to dim the clock thunders out three. A brief pause in darkness, during which we hear the White Friars of Death chanting a Mass from the nearby chapel. Then their voices fade and the clock strikes the half.

The lights come on. There is a pause. TOSCA *walks slowly from the bedroom. Her hair is rather tousled and she holds her earrings in her mouth. Otherwise she looks much as when we last saw her.* SCARPIA *follows her slowly on. He is clad now in a dressing-gown with the Baronial arms of* SCARPIA *on the left breast.*

I repeat, Tosca—it can only be something I ate.

TOSCA. Or perhaps you have been overworking. These late hours.

SCARPIA. Aie, Aie, Aieh! The shame of it, the pain of it!

TOSCA. Pain?

SCARPIA. Here,—in the very root of my being.

TOSCA. It could hardly be anywhere else.

SCARPIA. Ah, divine Tosca, I could smother you with my kisses, cover you with caresses—

TOSCA. You already have. (*Yawns.*) Kindly order me my carriage.

SCARPIA. No.

TOSCA. You are in the mood for conversation?

SCARPIA. A thousand curses!

TOSCA. Or perhaps a game of whist?

SCARPIA. Is it possible, my proud beauty, that you have forgotten that you are still in my power?

TOSCA. For what purpose?

SCARPIA. I can keep you here for as long as I wish. Oh yes, Tosca, here in these silent chambers, I can still wreak my will.

TOSCA. Your will? or your wont? Forgive me, Baron, for so poor a joke but the situation seems to permit some levity. To tell the the truth, I feel extremely sorry for you.

SCARPIA. I don't ask for your pity.

TOSCA. A shame, for it seems it is all I have to offer you, just at this moment. I have left my reticule upon your bed, and would like fully to repair such damage to my toilette as your recent transports have wreaked. Or is it wrought? When I return I shall expect to find a carriage waiting to take me to my home. Baron—

She makes a slight obeisance and goes out. SCARPIA *rings the the bell savagely. Then he sits at the desk. There are bangs and clatters at the door.* SCHIARRONE *comes in.*

SCHIARRONE. Excellency?

SCARPIA. There is a change of plan.

SCHIARRONE. (*Murmuring.*) Ah, this time I have brought a hand-kerchief.

SCARPIA. (*Loudly.*) We don't need a handkerchief. She isn't in the room—

TOSCA *can be heard off, singing* Vissi d'Arte *quietly to herself.*

SCHIARRONE. Nor she is. Good, it makes life easier. (*Referring to his notes.*) Now your Excellency will require a carriage for the Signora, having taken your pleasure of her, as per your dictated note, earlier.

SCARPIA. No, idiot! That's to say—no carriage—yet.

TOSCA *can be heard singing more loudly.*

SCHIARRONE. (*Surprised.*) Not yet?

He gets what is to him plainly the operative idea.

(*Admiringly.*) Eh, eh? Encora? Eh, eh, eh—?

SCARPIA. Not encora! Schiarrone, I must tell you something, in the strictest confidence—

SCHIARRONE. Your Excellency does me honour. (*He takes out his notebook.*)

SCARPIA. No notes! Heavens, if such notes were to fall into the hands of a Tribunal of Enquiry—

SCHIARRONE. Completely understood, Excellency. (*Notebook away.*) No names, no garotting—Excuse me. A Neapolitan Army expression.

TOSCA *is heard even more clearly.*

SCARPIA. The Signora Tosca has become a great danger to the state.

SCHIARRONE *has got lost in the glory of* TOSCA'S *voice.*

(*Sharply.*) Did you hear me, Schiarrone?

SCHIARRONE. Forgive me, Excellency, but what a divine voice the Signora does have. What is she singing about?

SCARPIA. Oh something about how she lived for art, lived for love—

SCHIARRONE. Oh yes. And she has. Oh, how she has—

SCARPIA. Well now she must die.

SCHIARRONE. Die?

SCARPIA. Die.

SCHIARRONE. Why?

SCARPIA. Because she has become possessed of a vital secret of state.

Pause.

SCHIARRONE. Classified?

SCARPIA. To the highest degree.

SCHIARRONE. King and Police chief only?

SCARPIA. Police chief only.

SCHIARRONE. Mama mia!

SCIARPIA. Mama, as you say, Schiarrone, mia! Now remembering that the Signora is a personal friend of the Queen, and a famous opera singer whose absence will be noted—how do we both set about it? Shall I have her shot beside her lover?

SCHIARRONE. Mario Cavaradossi? But isn't he to be shot by blanks?

SCARPIA. Balls, Schiarrone, balls.

SCHIARRONE. Oh yes. I'm so sorry. I have it here. Stupid of me. Real balls. *Not* blanks. See, Excellency, it is underlined—

SCARPIA. Yes. But she *thinks* they will be blanks—

TOSCA *is now into the closing phrases.*

Now supposing I told her that a famous painter was going to sketch the scene for posterity—say David—and how heroic and revoluntionary she would look, protecting her lover from the the cold lead balls of the Royalist murderers—how about that, eh, Schiarrone.

SCHIARRONE. Magnificent, Excellency. Only how will it be explained to the Queen?

Pause.

79

SCARPIA. As an accident. The firing party got confused between their blanks and their balls—

SCHIARRONE *looks doubtful.*

You don't like it? But, heavens, it *could* happen. The Queen of Naples must know her own subjects—

SHIARRONE. I think it might land Your Excellency in some rather difficult explanations. For instance why, in a straight-forward political execution, was blank ammunition ordered to be used anyway?

SCARPIA. Charitable reasons? To teach young Cavaradossi a lesson without actually harming him?

SCHIARRONE. Your Excellency's reputation is outstanding for many virtues—but whether charity is the most notable—

SCARPIA. All right, all right. What other way, then?

SCHIARRONE. Poison?

SCARPIA. In the Borgia apartments? That would not look good, Schiarrone. Not good at all.

SCHIARRONE. This vital secret, Excellency. Is it in her reticule?

SCARPIA. In her head.

SCHIARRONE. She has memorised it?

SCARPIA. Vividly. Or so I would think.

SCHIARRONE. That's bad. And it would, I imagine, be something like the Plans of the Central Fortifications?

SCARPIA. Or the lack of them, Schiarrone—which is far more serious—

SCHIARRONE. Deadly. Could You r Excellency perhaps plead with her better nature not to reveal this damaging in-adequacy?

SCARPIA. Am I in a position to appeal to her better nature about anything, Schiarrone?

SCHIARRONE. (*Thoughtfully.*) As her ravisher, you mean?

Pause.

SCARPIA. Ravisher is not a good word, Schiarrone. There are many other words for this kind of thing.

SCHIARRONE. (*Carried away.*) Like brutal possessor? Or proud and rampant conqueror?

SCARPIA. A precise definition is unnecessary and time-wasting. The point is simple : after tonight's events I doubt if I can exactly throw myself at the Signora's feet and plead for mercy—what are you grinning at, Schiarrone?

SCHIARRONE. The spectacle, that is all, Excellency—

SCARPIA. There is nothing to grin at, dolt. I deeply fear that La Tosca will have to be disposed of. Is that funny?

SCHIARRONE. A tragedy. (*Listening to her voice.*) Such purity of tone, such delicacy of feeling. You would never think, would you, that only minutes ago she was undergoing a fate that many women believe to be worse than death—

SCARPIA. It evidently takes different women different ways. (*Suddenly roaring.*) Idiot! Fool! Imbecile! Never mind about what's worse than death. Mind about death, and how to save La Tosca from it.

Pause.

SCHIARRONE. Would it be possible for you to render this dangerous secret inoperative?

SCARPIA. Inoperative?

SCHIARRONE. Your Excellency implied, just now, that what she has discovered was some structural failing in the Central Fortifications. Now is there perhaps some way in which Your Excellency might persuade her that what seemed to her, at first sight, a weakness was, on second sight, a strength.

Pause.

SCARPIA. By God, you may have hit on it, Schiarrone! Schiarrone, you may have the answer! Make it *inoperative*—weakness into strength—? (*He takes a sip of red wine.*) And it may well be done. The night, after all, is yet young. (*He looks at his watch.*) Well, youngish.

TOSCA'S *voice stops.*

She is coming out. Now listen, Schiarrone. Delay the execution by an hour—

SCHIARRONE. That will be well after daybreak, Excellency.

SCARPIA. Splendid. It will give the Firing Party a better chance to hit their target. (*Whispering.*) Or targets—Schiarrone—just in case this scheme of yours fails to work in the time allowed.

SCHIARRONE. (*Anxiously.*) Is the time enough, Excellency? You will surely have to construct a whole new imaginary set of plans—

SCARPIA. Oh, they won't be so imaginary, Schiarrone. I have a fairly solid base to work on . . . Fairly solid . . . I hope. Now before the hour is up I will call for you and give you your instructions.

SCHIARRONE. With a handkerchief?

SCARPIA. That signal has not proved infallible. For this, perhaps, a new one, something simpler. I know—if I am scowling at you, then the trick has not worked, and you will take the Signora down to the execution platform for a last adieu to her lover. Your firing party will then shoot them both. Understood?

SCHIARRONE. (*Writing.*) If they can hit them both.

SCARPIA. But if, as I hope, I am smiling at you, it will mean that all has gone as planned, and you will then have merely to summon a carriage and escort the Signora to her home. Now is that clear?

SCHIARRONE. As clear as crystal, Excellency. There is just one thing. Your Excellency's smile is a rather rare phenomenon. Might I be privileged to see one?

SCARPIA, with some effort, produces one. SCHIARRONE observes it carefully and then makes notes that long outlast the smile. (*Putting notebook away.*) I think I have it, Your Excellency. Carriage for smile, platform for scowl—

TOSCA *comes in from the bedroom.*

SCARPIA. (*Taking her hands.*) Dearest Diva, what bliss you have been giving us with that heavenly aria. What was it?

TOSCA. I was improvising—

SCARPIA. Of course. Ah, dear Tosca, you possess a truly magnificent organ.

Pause. It is only for a moment that TOSCA'S *eyes lower before meeting his again.*

TOSCA. Thank you, dear Baron. But even I have evenings when it is not quite at its peak. (*To* SCHIARRONE.) My carriage is here, Captain?

SCHIARRONE *looks frantically at* SCARPIA *who gives him a brusque shake of the head.* TOSCA *has gone to the window.*

SCHIARRONE. (*To* TOSCA'S *back.*) Yes, Signora—

SCARPIA. (*Hastily.*) The Captain means no Signora, it isn't here yet but it soon will be. Isn't that so, Captain?

SCHIARRONE. (*In a petulant whisper.*) But she's back in the room now—

SCARPIA *scowls at him.*

Oh, it is difficult. (*To* TOSCA.) Yes, Signora. I made a stupid blunder. Whatever Baron Scarpia said about your carriage is correct. It will be here whenever he says it's here.

SCARPIA. Go!

SCHIARRONE. (*Whispering.*) That means?

SCARPIA. Go! Get out! Leave!

SCHIARRONE. (*Getting the meaning.*) Ah. So much to do—so little time to do it? I understand. (*Saluting.*) Your Excellency.

SCARPIA. Captain.

SCHIARRONE *goes out.*

SCARPIA *goes up to* TOSCA, *who is still at the window. He tries to slip his arm round her waist.* Ah, my divine Tosca, what is there that I can say?

TOSCA *adroitly but not impolitely evades the encircling arm.*

TOSCA. In these circumstances surely nothing is always best.

SCARPIA. Always? You mean that such a thing has happened—

TOSCA. (*Interrupting severely.*) The experience is entirely new to me, Baron.

SCARPIA. Of course. How could it be otherwise?

TOSCA. How indeed? Nevertheless there are some ladies of my acquaintance—I move freely in the world as you know—to whom the event—or should I say non-event? Forgive me, Baron—is not wholly novel. There may, of course, be reasons for those misfortunes for which it would ill-become me to venture possible causes. However they all have without exception, told me that in such humiliating circumstances silence is best. Is that a lobster pâté?

SCARPIA. It is, dearest one.

TOSCA. And, dare I conjecture, a pork pie?

SCARPIA. A veal and egg pasty.

TOSCA. It will do. (*She sits down at the supper table, with authority.*)

SCARPIA *busies himself with serving her.*

After the dreadful ordeal to which tonight I have been submitted I feel a trifle weak and faint. A little food will do me good.

SCARPIA. (*Carving the pie.*) Do you, dearest heart, speak English?

TOSCA. No. It is a barbarous language. And they have no operas. Why should I speak it?

SCARPIA. It is just they have an expression— (*He puts a piece of pie before her.*) There. How is that? Now which wine?

TOSCA. A white, naturally, for the lobster. For the pie a drinkable red. I think you told me you had one. You made a bad joke about it being a good revolutionary year—'92—the year of the Terror. Also a very good vintage.

SCARPIA *displays a bottle. She inspects it.*

Yes—that must be the one. What is this expression that the English have?

SCARPIA. That you cannot have the best of two worlds. Either tonight you underwent an unspeakable ordeal, or there happened to you an non-event. Now which was it, because you really can't have it *both* ways?

There is a pause while TOSCA *masticates a mouthful of lobster pâté.*

TOSCA. (*At length.*) You are very direct, Baron . . . in your language . . . A little more of that white wine, if you would be so good—

SCARPIA *is so good.*

There happened to me tonight a non-event which was also an unspeakable ordeal. The English are quite wrong, you see. One can easily have it both ways, if one tries. (*She laughs gaily.*) SCARPIA *tries to follow her, and then falls grimly silent.*

SCARPIA. Ah, my Tosca—you see in me a very miserable man. I think the shame of tonight may very well be my end—

TOSCA. My dear Baron, you really must not take it so hard— (*correcting herself*) so much to heart. I am sure it is only a temporary affliction.

SCARPIA. Ah yes. So am I. If I thought otherwise I would hurl myself from that window this moment—

TOSCA. But dear Baron, pray pause for a moment to think. What you are speaking of is, after all, only a part of life—

SCARPIA. In the sense that ninety nine is only part of a hundred.

TOSCA. Surely you haven't forgotten that there is quite another kind of love, and that it is always referred to as the higher kind.

SCARPIA. (*Gloomily.*) I wonder why.

TOSCA. Because it *is* higher, Baron. Because it ennobles the soul and refreshes the spirit, and without it the whole world would be no more than a dungeon in the Castel Sant 'Angelo.—I think, now, I will try the red—

SCARPIA. (*Pouring.*) Is that the kind of love you have for Mario?

TOSCA *sips the red wine before replying.*

TOSCA. Not precisely, no. (*She sips again.*) I wish it were, but it is not. (*She sips once more.*) This is an excellent vintage. I congratulate you.

SCARPIA. Thank you. I knew you would like it. (*He pours her out a full glass.*)

84

TOSCA. (*After a pause.*) But it is the kind of love that Mario has for me.

SCARPIA. That amazes me.

TOSCA. Why does it?

SCARPIA. To be loved by the most desired and desirable woman in Rome, and not respond?

TOSCA. A lack of response is a relative term, Baron. As you should know. Mario does respond—in his fashion.

SCARPIA. What is his fashion?

TOSCA. Mario is not as other men. He is an idealist, a revolutionary, a poet—a man who has dedicated his whole life to the making of a better world.

SCARPIA. And does not that better world include a bed for the two of you?

Pause.

TOSCA. He confides to me most of his plans, Baron, but by no means all. Security you understand is very strict. I am close to Mario, of course, but in our little revolutionary circle, there are some who are even closer.

SCARPIA. Women?

TOSCA. Oh no. Men, naturally. Notably his very special friend, the young firebrand Angelotti. (*Hand over mouth.*) Oh dear— have I been indiscreet?

SCARPIA. The name is in our files.

TOSCA. I was sure it would be.

SCARPIA. He heads the Revolutionary Committee in Padua.

TOSCA. Really? I thought it was Mantua. But, of course, you would know better. Oh dear! My silly tongue! I really must keep a rein on it. I mean—just suppose—

SCARPIA. Have no fear, Signora. Our information on Angelotti, your Mario's bosom friend, needs no replenishing— (*Nevertheless he makes a brisk note at the desk.*) But I am appalled at this news you give me—that Mario is not as other men—

TOSCA. As most other men—But don't be appalled, Baron. I am not. I willingly accept my fate. I am not the first martyr to the glorious cause of Revolution—

SCARPIA. But, of course, you must have many other lovers, who are less high-minded, more—responsive—

TOSCA. Oh? Can you name me one?

Pause.

SCARPIA. Goodness, gracious me!

TOSCA. As you say, Baron—goodness, gracious you!

SCARPIA. But you were just singing—I lived for Art, I lived for Love—

TOSCA. A total absurdity. How can you live for both? You live for one, or you live for the other, and you make your choice too early in life to know whether you have chosen well. For an opera singer to have lovers in the sense in which you use the term—excuse me, Baron, but the vulgar sense—will make you late for rehearsals, quarrelsome with your castrati and uncertain in your top Cs. A Mario Cavaradossi, who looks very beautiful, has the noblest ideals and makes no demands upon you of any kind whatever is the only luxury that the disciplines of an opera singer's art can afford.

SCARPIA. Yet you say you love him differently? Physically, you meant—

TOSCA. That is my weakness. After all I am not a complete stranger to the less ascetic forms of love. As you may have noticed I am not actually—

SCARPIA. Yes.

TOSCA. A tenor in Assisi—a composer in Ischia. Both were quite unimportant. Mario has been my only true love—

SCARPIA. But shouldn't *true* love be the blissful conjunction of two souls in one perfect bodily union—(*He breaks off in some confusion*). I agree with you about this wine. It has an interesting maturity, and a certain flavour of the peaty earth—

TOSCA. (*Unkindly.*) Continue with your disquisition on true love, Baron. Coming from such a source it should be spellbinding.

SCARPIA. You are unkind.

TOSCA. Have I not the right to be?

SCARPIA. Yes. That does not make you less unkind.

TOSCA *reaches across the table and gently pats his hand.*

TOSCA. Forgive me. Let us talk of the wine—

SCARPIA. No. I accept the challenge. Disquisition on True Love. By Baron Scarpia—brutal and licentious Chief of Police to the hated Bourbons of Sicily—murderer and libertine. (*He gets up to begin pacing about, deep in thought, but with an occasional glance at his watch.*)

TOSCA. Do we need the introduction?

SCARPIA. Yes, we do. I am not by nature a murderer, nor a seducer. My reputation, which I freely grant, is the foulest in all Italy, is based on a total misconception.

Pause.

TOSCA. Baron, to whom are you speaking?

SCARPIA. (*Passionately, on his knees.*) To the woman I revere above all others, to the only woman I have ever loved.

TOSCA. As for reverence, Baron, you have a peculiar manner of showing it. And surely—although I don't wish to keep harping on the topic, a distinctly individual manner of displaying your love.

SCARPIA. (*On his knees.*) Ah, but don't you see, my beloved Tosca, it was precisely because of my reverence and my love that this evening became so humiliating a fiasco—

TOSCA. Excuse me, Baron, but if you would allow me one free hand?

He releases one, and she continues to eat her pork pie.

No harm possibly can come of your fondling the other.

SCARPIA *mutters an indistinct curse.*

Now explain to me the logic in what you have just said?

SCARPIA. Is there logic in love?

TOSCA. (*After reflection.*) Not much, no.

SCARPIA. If there were, would you love Mario Cavaradossi?

TOSCA. (*After reflection.*) No.

SCARPIA. Or would I love you?

TOSCA. (*After reflection.*) That is more difficult to answer. Just a touch more of that delicious Bourgogne, if you would be so kind.

He is so kind.

You have been good enough to say you loved and even revered me, and far be it from me to give the lie to a gentleman in his own Castello. But how can our two loves be compared. Mine for Mario is pure—

SCARPIA. And so is mine for you—

TOSCA. So indeed it proved.

SCARPIA. So it is. So it always has been. So it always will be. It was the truth that was proved tonight—(*The clock chimes.* SCARPIA *hastily compares the time with his own, and makes some adjustments*) Since I first saw you in Cherubini's 'Medea', I have been your worshipping slave, Tosca. Ah God, how I remember those three hours! It was January the twelfth, 1798 —and, ah the magic of you on that stage. From that moment on the vision of you as the tormented heroine filled the whole horizon of my life. I could think of nothing else. You became for me a mounting obsession—a maddening, torturing vision of love as it could be, of love as it should be, with all its pains and joys, its tribulations, its sacrifices and its joys—

TOSCA. Was it the matinee?

SCARPIA. No, the evening.

TOSCA. January the twelfth, 1798?... Ah yes, I remember. They put La Pizzoleta on for the matinee, because King Ferdinand was coming in the evening—

SCARPIA. And I came with him. I was in his box.

TOSCA. (*Very perfunctorily.*) Ferdinand! Brutal oppressor, murderer of the masses, fiend from hell. Did he say anything?

SCARPIA. That you were in splendid voice. But for me, Tosca, you became an ideal of radiance, of purity, of loveliness—just such a vision of womanhood in all its many-faceted beauty as I had felt might rescue me from the squalor and degradation into which my life was so rapidly sinking—

TOSCA. It's funny he didn't come round.

SCARPIA. Who?

TOSCA. King Ferdinand.

SCARPIA. The brutal oppressor, murderer of the masses—?

TOSCA. Yes, it's funny, that's all. Do go on.

SCARPIA. Well, you altered my whole existence. Until I saw and heard your glorious 'Medea' it is possible that my life might— who knows—have continued on its brutal and licentious path to hell. But after that never-to-be-forgotten night—

TOSCA. What made you such a villain?

SCARPIA. Opportunity, I think.

TOSCA. Without opportunity you would have been a simple, honest, god-fearing man?

SCARPIA. Can you doubt it?

TOSCA. (*Playfully.*) Frankly, Baron, I can.

SCARPIA. (*Passionately kneeling.*) Oh, don't doubt it, my beloved, I implore you. I beg you to believe that if it were not for my accursed office, I would be exactly the same as most other men.

TOSCA. That is rather easier to believe. But it is not at all the same question. Tell me then, Baron what made you seek your accursed office?

SCARPIA. Don't call me Baron. Call me Tonnino.

TOSCA. Why?

SCARPIA. It is my name.

TOSCA. Tonnino Scarpia?—I like it, it doesn't suit you at all, but

I like it. (*She strokes his hair playfully.*) Tell me, Tonnino, why did you ever allow yourself to become a Chief of Police?
Pause.

SCARPIA. (*Awaiting inspiration.*) To the hated Bourbons of Naples?

TOSCA. Yes.

Pause.

SCARPIA. And therefore a murderer and a libertine?

TOSCA. Yes.

Pause.

SCARPIA. That is a very good question.

TOSCA. Isn't it?

SCARPIA. The simplest answer I can give, off hand, is that it is an office that has to be filled, and that if I didn't fill it someone else would.

Pause.

TOSCA. Who might be an even worse murderer and a more brutal libertine than you?

SCARPIA. Beloved, you have exactly hit it.

TOSCA. I thought I had. (*She restrains belatedly the re-filling of her glass.*) No, please. I have an early rehearsal.

The clock thunders four.

How many times was that?

SCARPIA. Only four.

TOSCA. Oh good—*Four?*—

SCARPIA. (*Hastily.*) Beloved, I wish to make reparation to you for the dreadful humiliation I have inflicted on you earlier tonight a humiliation which it would take a lifetime to repay, but which it would take but a few brief minutes to repair.

Pause.

TOSCA. (*Gazing at him.*) What are you talking about?

SCARPIA. Your humiliation—my soul.

As she still seems forgetful, pointing.

In there, my dearest heart—

TOSCA *now finally does get it. She covers her face in an unsuccessful attempt to conceal her gleeful laughter.*

TOSCA. Oh yes—You couldn't do it.

SCARPIA. (*Sternly.*) I have already explained to you, light of my life, that it was my deep love for yourself as a woman, and my devoted reverence for you as an artist, that prevented that blissful conjunction between our twin souls and bodies that was surely ordained for us both by the gods.

Pause.
TOSCA. You explained that?
SCARPIA. At some length, beloved.
TOSCA. Did you? Aren't you clever?
SCARPIA. (*With a gesture.*) Come, my heart—
TOSCA. Where?
SCARPIA. In there.
TOSCA. Again?
SCARPIA. Come, oh constellation of my universe—
TOSCA. Do you know, dear Baron—
SCARPIA. Tonnino—
TOSCA. I think on the whole, I prefer Baron, I am not being
  unfriendly but it suits you better! I can only observe dear Baron
  —and this observation might, of course, be a little mellowed
  by your excellent red and white—but I can only observe that,
  had you made your overtures to me earlier this evening, in this
  vein, the outcome might have been much happier for both of
  us (*She ruffles his hair*) Tonnino! It's too silly. Would you
  kindly hand me my reticule?
SCARPIA *retrieves it from wherever it is and hands it to her.*
  While he is doing so TOSCA is staring at the ceiling.
TOSCA. There are cupids on your ceiling here, as well as in your
  bedroom.
SCARPIA. Yes, beloved.
TOSCA. How many are there here?
SCARPIA. Twenty six.
TOSCA. There are twenty-eight in the bedroom, isn't that correct?
SCARPIA. I have no idea. I have never counted them.
TOSCA. I have, quite a number of times. I am quite sure there
  are twenty-eight. Tiens, that is odd—twenty-six here, twenty-
  eight there. (*Out of her reticule she takes an elaborate, jewelled
  engagement book.*) Dear Baron, I think another visit to that
  room tonight would be inadvisable for both of us. I have an
  early rehearsal, you are as you have admitted not quite yourself, and the night is late. In fact it is no longer night. See (*She
  points to the window*) where jocund day stands tiptoe on the
  misty mountain tops . . . Romeo and Juliet . . . I suppose that
  absurd little farce with Mario and those blank cartridges will
  soon have to be enacted down there. Now what evening can
  I possibly fit you in? . . .
She looks through her engagement book and, not getting an

answer from SCARPIA, *looks up sharply*). Wasn't it to be at dawn?

SCARPIA. (*Uneasily.*) Dawn or dawn-abouts.

TOSCA. I thought these things were always at dawn.

SCARPIA. There is a little—elasticity—

TOSCA. Well, anyway, Mario goes to Milan today. You have made arrangements for his journey?

SCARPIA. I—er—think everything is in hand—

TOSCA. Only *think*?

SCARPIA. Dear Tosca, I have had so much else on my mind. . . .

TOSCA. Yes, I suppose you have. Well we will make quite sure of all that in a minute. I shall want to talk to that young Captain myself. He seems a type who could rather easily be confused. Don't you agree?

SCARPIA. Fervently.

TOSCA. Now, with Mario gone to Milan I could write you down for next Thursday. That is the night of the great gala at the Opera. 'Medea', as, by a coincidence, it happens—Isn't that nice?

SCARPIA. Nice is hardly the word.

TOSCA. I am invited afterwards to the Royal Palace, and you can be my escort.

SCARPIA. That would be wonderful, beloved, but—dare I confess it—a night at the Royal Palace was not exactly what I had in mind.

TOSCA. What you have in mind, Baron, by tonight's events or even non-events, has been quite firmly implanted in my own. Never fear, caro Tonnino . . . No, I'm afraid it *must* be Baron . . . But never fear, on Thursday evening everything will go quite *swimmingly.* You have my guarantee (*Inspecting her engagement book before putting it away.*) Yes, Thursday is a good evening for me, Baron—for even if Mario had been available he would not have been a persona exactly gratissima at the Royal Palace.

SCARPIA. Seeing that his plan was to blow it up?

Pause. TOSCA *momentarily loses her calm.*

TOSCA. Your agents know even that?

SCARPIA. One did.

TOSCA. But that plan was known only to me.

SCARPIA. And one other—

TOSCA. (*Without utter misery.*) Ah! Angelotti? It was Angelotti, then who betrayed him? Oh fiend, Oh devil, Oh thrice—accursed traitor! When Mario hears of this—as he shall—have no fear—

SCARPIA. Angelotti did not betray him.

TOSCA. Oh? He didn't? Well, then who did?

SCARPIA. To what other person did your Mario tell his plot?

TOSCA. No one.

SCARPIA. No one at all?

TOSCA. Well, naturally, to the agents of Fouché—

SCARPIA. Aha!

Pause.

TOSCA. *(Aghast).* What you are suggesting is too vile to be believed—

SCARPIA. Nothing in this world. Tosca, is too vile to be believed. This is the year 1800, Signora, and we live in a cesspit—a world that has gone mad—

TOSCA. Not—Fouché—

SCARPIA. Fouchê.

TOSCA. Betrayed my Mario?

SCARPIA. And all his accomplices.

TOSCA. The first consul of France shall know of this.

SCARPIA. The first consul of France does know of it.

He produces a document from his tunic pocket the one he once briefly flourished as a death warrant.

Do you read that signature?

TOSCA. *(In a whisper.)* Bonaparte. *(She kisses it passionately.)* Oh Bonaparte! My idol! My love! My inspiration! *(She kisses it again, then rubs the document with a napkin.)* A touch of lobster pâté. *(Reading.)* A Monsieur le Baron Scarpia, Chef de Police de Sa Majesté, Le Roi Ferdinand . . . Mon cher ami . . . *(Appalled.)* Mon cher ami?

SCARPIA. *(Snatching the document back.)* There is much in this that must not be read, even by you—my beloved—or it will cost both of us our heads. Here is the relevant part: "Regarding the Jacobin conspirators of whom my Chief of Police Fouché has afforded you a comprehensive list, by far the most dangerous is Mario Cavaradossi, a known firebrand and revolutionary, and a suspected homos—" I need not read you that particular passage—"This Cavaradossi's plan to explode the Royal Palace shows a wanton disregard for the sacred laws of property which I, as First Consul of Revolutionary France

92

cannot and will not countenance. Apart from causing irreparable damage to a historic building in which, one day, I might hope to reside, it could also have destroyed some very valuable paintings which I still need for my collection. Mario Cavaradossi must be shot out of hand—and at once.

TOSCA *has appeared about to faint.* SCARPIA *hurries to her side with a glass of wine.*

TOSCA. Ah, Baron—would that you had ravished my body, rather than my soul!

SCARPIA. Would that I had too. I mean, I quite agree. I really am most awfully sorry to have had to break it to you this way dear Tosca. Would you care for a little brandy?

TOSCA. Yes.

SCARPIA *goes to get it.*

(*Murmuring.*) 'Oh villain, most perfidious villain! Oh monster among men'.

SCARPIA. (*His back to her.*) Me?

TOSCA. No, Bonaparte.

He returns with the brandy.

What, after all, are *you* but Bonaparte's jackal?

SCARPIA. (*Sitting.*) Well at least that's better than being King Ferdinand's jackal, isn't it?

TOSCA. So you are two jackals—

SCARPIA. Yes but for the price of one. I only get paid by King Ferdinand.

TOSCA. Oh what a terrible life you lead!

SCARPIA. It's a terrible world. All I have done is to take out a little insurance on the future.

TOSCA. My ideals are utterly shattered.

SCARPIA. (*Joining her in a brandy.*) Oh dear! Yes, I suppose they must be.

TOSCA. Poor Mario! what is to become of him?

SCARPIA. Well—that is rather a question, isn't it?

TOSCA. Ring the bell.

SCARPIA. Yes, beloved. (*He does so.*)

TOSCA. But to what purpose is this farce of a mock execution? Mario will surely die anyway.

SCARPIA. Well, of course, with a Neapolitan firing squad, accidents can always happen.

TOSCA. I mean he will die of shame and disillusionment.

SCARPIA. Well, better disillusioned than dead,—that's what I always say. Or don't you agree?

SCHIARRONE *has entered.* SCARPIA *confronts him with the customary scowl. Evidently he has forgottten the new signals.* Now Schiarrone—listen carefully—

SCHIARRONE. (*After searching* SCARPIA's *face carefully.*) Yes. The Signora is to be taken down to the platform where she is to bid adieu to her lover—

SCARPIA. (*Murmuring.*) No, Schiarrone—

SCHIARRONE. (*Undeterred.*) While the firing squad level their muskets at them both—

SCARPIA. (*Murmuring again.*) Not exactly, Schiarrone—

SCHIARRONE. And the muskets of course, are to be loaded with blanks, not balls. Never fear, Excellency. I have the whole thing pat.

He looks pleased with himself. SCARPIA *does not look pleased with him.*

SCARPIA. (*Now really scowling.*) You have not got it pat, Schiarrone. Not pat at all. I will now try to make it pat—

TOSCA. (*Who has not been listening.*) May I speak to the Captain?

SCARPIA. By all means, dearest one.

TOSCA. Captain, what arrangements have you made for conveying Signor Cavaradossi from this place after the business with the firing squad?

Pause.

SCHIARRONE. I had arranged a conveyance, Signora.

TOSCA. What kind of conveyance?

SCHIARRONE. (*After a helpless look at* SCARPIA.) A suitable conveyance.

TOSCA. For a long journey?

SCHIARRONE. Very long.

SCARPIA. The Signora means, will it take him to *Milan*? (*He pulls out a handkerchief with a flourish, and drops it.*) Ah, how careless—

TOSCA *has pounced on the handkerchief in a trice, and uses it to press to her eyes.*

TOSCA. Milan! Milan! and Bonaparte! Accursed fiends! Ah, how my heart breaks, how my eyes swim with the memories of my shattered ideals!

She puts the handkerchief in her reticule watched by both SCARPIA *and* SCHIARRONE.

94

We must not send him to any place within reach of his mortal enemy. And yet Bonaparte bestrides the world. Where then may we send him? (*To* SCHIARRONE.) This conveyance that you have ordered for him? Does it go at a fast pace?

SCHIARRONE. Not—usually—

TOSCA. How fast? Would it, for instance, reach Venice by nightfall?

SCHIARRONE. (*Appalled.*) *Venice?*

SCARPIA. I fancy you have made a small error, haven't you Schiarrone, in your ordering of this conveyance for Signor Cavaradossi?

SCHIARRONE. (*Resigned.*) I wouldn't be at all surprised.

SCARPIA. The conveyance that the Captain has ordered for Mario is I imagine rather cumbersome, and accustomed only to *local* journeys. Isn't that so, Captain?

SCHIARRONE. (*Almost mutinous.*) And it takes it at a rather funereal pace—if the Signora follows me—

SCARPIA. (*Muttering.*) If she did you'd be dead. (*He pats* SCHIARRONE'S *shoulder.*) Now what we need, Schiarrone, is a vehicle that proceeds at a much more lively pace. Understand? Something that might, for instance, get Signore Cavaradossi—alive and well, Schiarrone, alive and well, remember—to Leghorn before dawn.

TOSCA. Leghorn?

SCARPIA. The British Fleet is there, and Mario as an enemy of Bonaparte, can take refuge on a British warship and be given passage to England.

TOSCA. England? But as a known revolutionary he will be shot by King George.

SCARPIA. Oh no. Far more likely he will be invited to Carlton House, as a guest of the Prince of Wales. (*Affably, to* SCHIARRONE.) Now I trust, Schiarrone, we have cleared up any little confusion you might still have had about this morning's work?

SCHIARRONE *desperately searches his notes.*

SCARPIA *brusquely tears off a page and scribbles something in pencil.*) But just in case we haven't—you did say you wanted it all in writing, didn't you? Safer, I think you said, that way. (*He hands it to* SCHIARRONE.)

SCHIARRONE. (*At great length.*) No—balls?

SCARPIA. (*Smiling.*) Precisely.

SCHIARRONE. No balls at all?

SCARPIA. None at all.

As SCHIARRONE *ponders the note* SCARPIA *puts his arm on* SCHIARRONE'S *shoulder again.*

SCARPIA. You realise, I hope, that if you bring this night's work to a successful conclusion, you may well receive promotion?

SCHIARRONE. A Major? Me? But I'd have to grow a moustache.

SCARPIA. I have no doubt that even that is not beyond your capabilities.

Suddenly we hear a tolling of a bell and the sound of muffled drums. SCARPIA *dashes to the window.*

Oh my god, they're marching him out already, what is the meaning of this, Schiarrone?

SCHIARRONE. Well, they shouldn't be marching him out, I mean, I'm their Captain, and they ought to have waited for me. The thing is, of course, they're used to shooting people at dawn and if they're late home their wives get jealous—

SCARPIA. Call to them from the window—

TOSCA. (*At the window.*) Ah, there is my Mario! How brave and proud he looks! A King among mortals. A Committee Chairman among his Board—

SCARPIA. Shout to them, Schiarrone.—

SCHIARRONE. There is no need to get panicky. Excellency, they are my own men. They can and will do nothing without *me*. (*Shouting from the window.*) My brave men! This is your Captain, Captain Schiarrone—

He is greeted by a ragged, loud and rather drunken cheer. He doesn't seem to be unpopular—but nor does he seem to have exerted over his brave men an absolutely iron discipline. There are several loud and very coarse comments on the identity of the lady framed in the window with him, and on her reasons for being there. TOSCA *hasn't helped by calling melodiously to her lover.*

TOSCA. Mario! Mario! Mario!

SCHIARRONE. My gallant children I love you all, as you love me. Think always of the glory and fame of the Kingdom of the Two Sicilies—

There is a sound that (forty years ago) would have been described as a 'raspberry'.

And of our beloved King Ferdinand, in whose sacred cause we pledge our lives—

96

Dead silence, broken by TOSCA, *in melodious voice.*

TOSCA. Mario, Mario, Mario!!! Oh, my Mario—why do you not look at me?

There is instant cheering. The soldiers are evidently uncertain about exactly whom she is shouting to, but delighted that it is not to anyone called Ferdinand.

SCHIARRONE. (*Shouting through the window.*) Loyal sons of Naples, I your Captain, command you to unload your muskets!

There is the sound of a volley.

SCARPIA. Oh my god!

SCHIARRONE. Don't fret, Excellency. That's their way of unloading their muskets, it's just high spirits. No one was hurt—(*Looking down.*) I think. (*Shouting.*) Well done, my brave men. Now I personally, your Captain, will descend to give you your orders. Do nothing whatever until I reach your side.

There is another raspberry and a crash of muskets to the ground.

TOSCA. (*Calling plaintively.*) Mario! Mario! He will not even turn his head. And yet he must have recognised my voice. Oh, what has happened?

SCHIARRONE. I think I can explain that, Signora. Signor Cavaradossi has heard that you have spent some hours in the Baron's chambers—

TOSCA. Who has betrayed me?

SCHIARRONE. The White Friars of Death. They are inclined to a little gossip between executions. (*To* SCARPIA.) Excellency, about an hour ago, Signor Cavaradossi told me that he would not purchase his life at the price of Signora Tosca's honour.

SCARPIA *looks at* TOSCA. *Pause.*

SCARPIA. His life is not now at stake.

SCHIARRONE. Oh no, but when it *was*—you know when it was going to be a fake *fake* execution—Your Excellency will understand what I mean—and I gave Cavaradossi his instructions which of course were fake too, then—to fall down at the sound of the volley, I mean—which then wouldn't have been fake at all—are you still with me, Excellency?

SCARPIA. (*Menacingly.*) Ahead of you, Schiarrone.

SCHIARRONE. Well, Signor Cavaradossi told me then that he would *not* fall down at the sound of the volley, and that no one could get him to fall down. He would remain standing, he said, shouting revolutionary slogans, and singing the Marseillaise, until they did shoot him. He was quite insistent.

97

SCARPIA. Why did you not tell me this before?

SCHIARRONE. Well at the time, the question of whether or not Signor Cavaradossi remained standing seemed of comparatively minor importance. (*He laughs.*) But now, of course, it's different. Oh dear, what are we to do?

SCARPIA. Blindfold the firing party!

TOSCA. (*Intervening calmly.*) No, Baron. Dear Baron, there is only one thing to do. Mario must be told the truth.

SCARPIA. The naked truth?

TOSCA. If that is how it can be described.

SCARPIA. Ah no, Tosca. Not that! Anything but that— (*He kneels at her feet.*) I implore you—save me from this shame, this horror, this degradation—pity me, Tosca—oh pity me!

TOSCA. I do pity you, Baron, as you know—but I cannot allow my Mario to go to his exile under the load of a gross and hideous misunderstanding.

SCARPIA *moans.*

Baron, are you man enough? Are you what I think you might yet be?

SCARPIA *gets to his feet, squares his shoulders and faces SCHIARRONE.*

SCARPIA. Schiarrone, you may assure the prisoner, on the word of Baron Scarpia, that the honour of Signora Tosca is safe, and has been these last two hours.

Pause.

SCHIARRONE. Non e vero . . . !

SCARPIA. E vero.

SCHIARRONE. But—Excellency . . . (*He points to* SCARPIA'S *attire.*).

SCARPIA. The Signora was prepared to make the sacrifice, but I did not find myself in a position to accept it.

SCHIARRONE. Your Excellency is just surely having his fun?

SCARPIA. (*Thunderously.*) No, you baboon, he is not having his fun. Nor has he had it—And that is the point—

SCHIARRONE. (*Beginning to giggle.*) Il Barone Scarpia!—Il famoso Monstro di Roma!—Il fabulose Barone Scarpia!—(*He doubles up.*)

SCARPIA. (*Quietly.*) I can very easily organise another firing-party, Schiarrone—this time with grape-shot.

SCHIARRONE. (*Instantly sobering.*) Excellency.

SCARPIA. Go and give that message to Signore Cavaradossi. And then take yourself out of my sight—forever.

SCHIARRONE. But the carriage for La Tosca?

SCARPIA. Yes. Arrange that, and then announce it. But after that I never wish to see your face again. Do you understand?

SCHIARRONE. Your Excellency cannot be so unkind.

TOSCA. (*Coming forward.*) Dearest, it is not the mark of a great soul to impute blame for the waywardness of events to a young and wholly innocent party. Captain, I am grateful for your part in the happenings of the past hours, and I promise you that such influence as I may be able to exert upon the Baron will not be wasted on your behalf.

SCHIARRONE. The Signora is too kind.

TOSCA. Pray go and attend to the execution of my beloved. Oh, and many congratulations on your promotion.

SCHIARRONE. Signora!

TOSCA. (*Thoughtfully.*) Yes. A moustache would suit you very well.

SCHIARRONE. Oh Signora—(*Bowing.*) Your Excellency. (*He goes gravely, but his gravity does not outlast his journey to the door. Before the bolts and bars clang into place we hear a shrill peal of youthful laughter. As he goes.*) Il Barone Scarpia! Impotente! Non e possibile! Non e vero! Eh, eh, eh! Impotente! Il Barone Scarpia!

SCARPIA *grimly faces* TOSCA.

TOSCA. You have done most nobly, Baron, and I am proud of you. Now, at last, you have persuaded me that there is some hope for your spiritual regeneration.

Pause.

SCARPIA. At the hands of a good woman?

TOSCA. How else could it come to so villainous a man?

SCARPIA. How indeed? But what about my physical regeneration?

TOSCA. That too will come.

SCARPIA. Also at the hands of a good woman?

TOSCA. Who knows, Baron? Life after all, has its constant surprises—And, in life, is there any thing more surprising than love? And the many, many forms it can take? That, at least, is what I always say—

SCHIARRONE'S *voice can be heard barking orders from the platform below.*

Shall we watch? It should be fun—

They go to together to the window.

Ah look. Your Captain is giving my Mario your message—

There is a sudden, loud, tenor's laugh from outside.

That was a little vulgar. Not like a true Revolutionary—I must speak to him—when I get the chance.

More barked orders from SCHIARRONE *down below. The drums begin to beat again.*

MARIO. (*Off, singing in a high tenor.*)

Allons, enfants de la Patrie!
Le jour de gloire est arrivé
Contre nous de la tyrannie
L'étendard sanglant—

A barked order from SCHIARRONE.

est levé

L'étendard sanglant est. . . .

The voice is cruelly cut off—and, it seems, perpetually silenced by by a volley of musket fire. There is dead stillness for a moment, before we hear more barked orders from SCHIARRONE, *and the sound of the soldiers retreating.*

TOSCA. Ah, how magnificently he fell! One could have almost sworn it was real. Don't you agree, Baron?

SCARPIA. (*A shade anxiously.*) One could have almost sworn it.

TOSCA. The Captain is now telling him it is safe to rise.

There is a long pause.

What is that on Mario's forehead? Is it, can it be, don't tell me—blood?

SCARPIA. It does look a little like blood.

TOSCA. Ah—Viper, toad, devil! Ten times accursed fiend—

She brings off one of the most spectacular faints in theatrical history.

SCARPIA *is too preoccupied to do more than throw her prostrate body a glance.*

SCARPIA. Schiarrone—what has gone wrong down there?

SCHIARRONE. (*Off.*) A little accident, Excellency—

SCARPIA. I can see that from up here, idiot—

SCHIARRONE. (*Off.*) I think the prisoner fainted at the sound of the volley and hit his head—ah yes. He is recovering, Excellency. See. (*Evidently to* MARIO.) One, two, three and oops! There we are! No harm done. Now we'll just get you to this coach, because you're off to Leghorn and England—

MARIO. (*Agonised, off.*) Oh no! Not England! Why didn't you kill me!

Meanwhile SCARPIA *has run to the inert body of* TOSCA *and has*

100

lifted it with some difficulty, placing it tenderly on a couch.

SCARPIA. (*Patting her face.*) Tosca! . . . Tosca! . . . Come to. All is well.

But she remains lifeless. Distraught he tears some feathers from her fan, goes to the candle, lights them, and holds them under her nose—burning his fingers in the process, and uttering an oath. TOSCA *opens her eyes.*

TOSCA. What is that terrible smell?

SCARPIA. Feathers—you fainted—

TOSCA. (*Remembering.*) Ah monster—jackal—spawn of Satan—

SCARPIA. But Mario is not dead. He is safe, beloved—

TOSCA. (*Ruefully.*) But my best fan—

SCARPIA. I shall give you ten others, far better—

He has found himself in an extremely amorous position. Not to mince words you might say that he is now, physically at least, on top.

TOSCA. Oh no, not ten. Ten is ridiculous. . . . The name of the shop is Marocchetti, in the Via Boccaccio—

SCARPIA. I shall remember, beloved one.

He has managed to untie the cord of his dressing-gown.

TOSCA. And you will not forget either, will you dear Baron, the promises you made me about seeking, in future, only the higher forms of love—

SCARPIA. How could I forget them, my divine Tosca? My life, from now on, will be a model of spirituality and good form—

His dressing-gown slips off without apparent difficulty. He kisses her passionately. She does not resist. Then gently he begins to undress her.

TOSCA. (*After a pause.*) Twenty-eight cupids, you say?

SCARPIA. No, beloved. Twenty-six. Twenty-eight in the bedroom—

TOSCA. (*Dreamily.*) I think I prefer twenty-six. (*She has been nearly undressed.*)

SCHIARRONE *strides briskly in. He has on a travelling cloak, and is putting on gloves. For the first time in the whole evening he looks supremely confident. This time he knows he has got it right.*

SCHIARRONE. Your Excellency? . . . (*He looks round the room.*) Your Excellency? . . . I am happy to tell you that the Signora's carriage awaits her.

Pause.

SCARPIA. (*From the couch.*) Yes, Schiarrone. That is clever of you. You will now send it away, and instruct it to return at dawn.

SCHIARRONE. (*Aggrieved.*) But it is dawn . . .

SCARPIA. No. It will not be dawn until I make it—

SCHIARRONE. And when will that be, Excellency?

SCARPIA. Quite soon, I think. . . . Perhaps even very soon. . . . But not just yet. Go! I will ring for you.

SCHIARRONE. Yes, Excellency. (*He goes towards the door, then stops, as a thought strikes him. He takes out the inevitable notebook.* Can Your Excellency give me some idea of how long I shall have to wait?

SCARPIA. (*Looking at* TOSCA.) A lifetime. . . .

SCHIARRONE. (*Taking his note.*) A lifetime? I thank Your Excellency. I have your meaning, I hope.

SCARPIA. I hope I have it myself. Go!

SCHIARRONE *puts his notebook away, salutes and goes.*

TOSCA. (*Muttering.*) Twenty-two, twenty-three, twenty-four, twenty—

Her lips are closed by SCARPIA'S *before she has completed the full count.*

THE LIGHTS FADE

102